HOW TO

SLAY A
PIRATE

LESSONS ON SUCCESS
FROM SAILING THE PACIFIC

Barbara E. Gottesman, LL.B., CPCC, ACC

HOW TO SLAY A PIRATE
LESSONS ON SUCCESS FROM SAILING THE PACIFIC
Barbara E. Gottesman, LL.B., CPCC, ACC

Copyright © 2013
Berkeley Avenue Press
ISBN-13: 978-0615898865
ISBN-10: 0615898866"

Cover photograph by Harrison Mitgang.
Author photograph by Paula Beemer and Beemer Studios (www.beemerstudios.com).
All rights reserved.

Printed in the United States of America

DEDICATION

This book is dedicated to my husband and fearless captain, without whom this journey may never have happened, and to my courageous children, who remind me each and every day never to settle for less.

This book is also dedicated to dream seekers everywhere—and especially to those who are committed to taking the leap to make those dreams a reality.

HOW TO SLAY A PIRATE:
Lessons on Success from Sailing the Pacific

Twenty years from now you will be more disappointed by the things that you didn't do than by the ones you did do. So throw off the bowlines. Sail away from the safe harbor. Catch the trade winds in your sails. Explore. Dream. Discover.

-Mark Twain

ONE YEAR AGO

The 2010 Baja Haha, an annual cruisers' rally from San Diego to Cabo San Lucas, is departing today, Monday, October 25, 2010. We were registered to leave with this rally in 2009, along with nearly 200 other boats, but because of some unexpected health issues, we decided to postpone our departure. Health issues, or the possibility of them, are one of the reasons for doing this trip. Michael and I both lost our fathers at very young ages (his dad was 61, mine was 54). But these new issues, which turned up only 10 days before our planned departure, put us into a new conundrum. What were we to do? Should we even go at all? A lifetime of dreams, painful decision making, grueling planning and preparations, and high expectations were all at stake.

After balancing out all the risks and worst-case scenarios, we decided to wait out only a couple of weeks, which put our departure only 3 days later than the rest of the HaHa fleet. Our crew members were flexible enough to leave late with us. We were still able to check in with the fleet every morning once we got started, and caught up at both stops before meeting again in time for the Big Party upon arrival in Cabo San Lucas.

But, of course, we questioned our actions every step of the way. Were we being irresponsible? Selfish? Foolish? Would we be able to forgive ourselves if something did happen?

And here we are, one year later. The health issues that delayed us in the first place have all but faded, while many incredible experiences are behind us. Did we do the right thing? Given how things turned out, we can easily say we did, but had it been different, who knows?

I guess that's the thing. Who's to say one decision is better than another? A decision just is. And then you go with it...

Should we be doing another year? Should we be going to Central America or to the South Pacific? Should we haul our boat in La Paz or in Mazatlan for a bottom paint? Should we meet guests in Zihuatenajo or in Huatulco? How long can we wait for a "weather window?" When should we be making our crossing to Mazatlan from La Paz? We consider our options, talk it through, make a decision and then go with it. We cannot look back. We must look ahead. And if changes need to be made, we make them as yet another decision in our path.

In fact, that's a huge lesson that cruising teaches you. You cannot get bogged down in the what-ifs, or you won't do anything. You consider your options, you make your decisions, you go with it until the next decision needs to get made. That's life, isn't it? Only in the cruising world, the decisions seem so exaggerated, somehow; perhaps because each one is so all-encompassing to your life at that moment, or perhaps it's that some have a real bearing on your personal safety, or maybe it's because they need to be made so often. Or am I forgetting what it's like to live on land?

I am grateful that we've been in good health for the last year. And we'll keep looking ahead.

-Barbara, signing off from La Paz, BCS, Mexico

INTRODUCTION:
Navigation to Adventure

You cannot discover new oceans unless you have the courage to lose sight of the shore.

-Andre Gide (1869-1951)
French Author, Nobel Prize in Literature 1947

On April 1, 2009, at the height of the global financial crisis, my husband, who had worked in the financial services industry for nearly 20 years, came home, helped me put the kids to bed, and unloaded his first bombshell of that year: He lost his job. Two weeks later, with a grim economic outlook, he came home with the second bombshell: We should rent out our house, buy a boat, and go sailing with the kids for a year. Just like that.

My immediate reaction: I don't know how to sail. I hate the water. I can't even help my kids with their homework without World War III breaking out, let alone homeschooling them. My kids, like most siblings, don't always get along, and I couldn't imagine how much more difficult it would be for all of us to get along in really small quarters.

Without a pause, my mind continued to protest. We had never been on an overnight passage. The longest sailing trip we had ever taken was four days and three nights from Santa Cruz to Monterey and back again. I'm prone to seasickness. I loved my work as a life, career, and executive coach, I loved my clients, and I couldn't imagine giving that up.

In other words, my answer was a resounding "NO."

So how was it that, within five months, my husband, Michael, and I found ourselves the owners of *Whatcha Gonna Do*, a 46-foot catamaran, and had rented out our home and moved aboard our first-ever boat at a shipyard in San Diego? It was just the four of us—me, my husband, and our two children, Danielle (then 11) and Harrison (then 8)—living at a dock in a *really* small space with *really* big plans for a sailing sabbatical. And, within six weeks of moving aboard, how did we get to setting sail for points south for a year of adventure in Mexico that turned into two-and-a-half years and included the longest ocean passage in the world and nearly 7,000 miles of cruising through the South Pacific to Australia?

The leap from a definite "No!" to an intrepid "Yes" came because several things were gnawing at me right from the beginning. I was a life coach, helping people to live their dreams, and yet I was going to let my husband's dream of a sailing sabbatical wither away. How could I not do this with him? It wasn't like I was afraid of travel. I've been adventure traveling my whole life: Europe, Thailand, Turkey, Israel, Nepal, India, and Peru.

Through my own introspection, I soon realized that I, too, had a dream. Mine was to travel with my children and show them that there is so much more out there in this vast and diverse world beyond the socio-economically middle-class privileged bubble they were living in. When Michael put a voice to his dreams, it made me see that I hadn't even allowed my own dream to enter my radar screen. How could that be?

As I watched my husband peruse the Boats for Sale websites, I decided I needed to examine what was really stopping *me*. I had to be sure the decision I was making at this point in my life was going to be one based on truths, not on fears. I had to figure out if my "No" was a result of my own dissonance or my fears.

One by one, I pulled apart my truths. I enrolled in a sailing course and realized I actually knew more than I thought I did from years of sailing with Michael, tacking, raising sails, hauling lines, and docking. While he continued to study the Boats for Sale websites, I started perusing the homeschooling sites. I saw that there were many families out there homeschooling and many cruising families doing it with programs that were either self-designed or not Internet-dependent (which would be necessary for when we were offshore or in places without Internet access). We planted the seed in our kids' minds and saw that they were so excited that they were able to hypothesize and dream *together* about what they'd see and do if they were to live on a boat. Plus, I knew there was medication available to alleviate sea sickness, and once you've lived on a boat for a few days, you'll get your sea legs and fend off sea sickness eventually. As for my life coaching practice, what better advertisement is there than really walking my talk?

So there I was, having pushed myself out of my comfort zone, my element, everything I knew, into something wholly different. What made it even more remarkable was *how far* I was out of my element. I wasn't used to pushing myself to that degree. I was scared to death, and excited and elated, all at the same time.

Undoubtedly, I feel at the top of my game and most alive when I successfully get through stretching myself beyond what even I thought possible. There aren't many who choose to take a sabbatical, and even fewer who do it by sailing into the sunset—with their families. Yes, stretching myself was putting it mildly. This was going far beyond routine. Was it going to be too much?

Sunday, May 29, 2011

LIVING ON THE EDGE

It's not uncommon, based on my unscientific poll, for women to feel "on the edge" while cruising. It's not the adventure type of living on the edge, but rather the type that has you ridiculously happy and fulfilled one moment and then completely anxious or snappy or melancholy the next. There's no reason to feel low, and I'm sure it's tough for many to feel my pain. But it's still an interesting phenomenon from strictly a psychological perspective.

I do wonder why I am not on a constant "happy ride." After all, I'm in paradise, with my family, traveling and experiencing incredible things. As I've mentioned before, though, it's hard work. Just going to the grocery store is a full day event. And things break. All the time. And there's dirt everywhere. All the time. And it's been raining—no, pouring torrentially—for the last few days, and the wind is gusting to such an extent that it has overturned dinghies in our anchorage. And I'm just plain tired of it. I have never felt like such an inadequate housekeeper as now.

One theory is that, as cruisers, we stretch ourselves beyond our comfort zones every day. At first, it's exhilarating, knowing you can get through it. But after a while, it's simply exhausting. I'd love to get off for just a few days—take a shower with hot water and not worry about how much I'm using, and not have to press the shower pump button to get the water to go down the drain. I'd like to live in a clean house without sunscreen fingerprints and oily salt. I'd like to be able to go for lunch with my girlfriends for something other than raw fish in coconut milk. I'd like to be able to wake up in the middle of the night in a storm and not worry about whether our anchor is dragging or our hatches are closed or if there's a leak somewhere that will cause ugly mold to appear. I'd like to be able to go to the grocery store and buy whatever I feel like eating, and for only a regular week's worth of produce—and not worry that it will have to last me for four weeks. I want a kitchen that fits more than one person in it. I want space. I'd like to be able to send my kids to school and let the teachers worry about whether they are developing academically as they should be. I want to feel dry and clean. I want to have all my laundry done at one time. I want to be able to relax. I want some familiarity. This newness is driving me, well, over the edge.

                                                    -Barb

Still on 'Ua Pou, Iles de Marqueses, French Polynesia;
setting out this afternoon for Makemo Atoll, in the
Tuamotu Archipelago

By the end of the adventure, after living on the edge, what I came out with was a belief that I could actually do it and an inspiration to keep going beyond what I thought was possible. I also quickly realized that the hardest thing of all was simply taking the leap, literally, throwing off the dock lines. Once we had jumped (or rather left the dock), the rest felt relatively easy. And while our change was perhaps close to being as radical as we could get for our family, once we had begun our journey, we felt refreshed and confident that we could actually take on much, much more. I have undoubtedly become far bolder.

Just as it was important for me, it was crucial that my kids recognized how enriching taking a leap can be and that they really understood that they could direct their lives to wherever their hearts (and compasses) were pointing.

Our family's journey before and during this sailing adventure led me to look closer at what it takes to make a leap such as this, a leap into doing what you really want to be doing, into living the ultimate dream that you've had on your mind for what seems like forever, but which somehow never felt attainable. I dissected the steps that are essential, first, to believing that it can be done, and then, to taking your own leap.

I realized that perhaps the most important obstacle that stands between you and living your dreams or making a leap toward living according to your purpose is actually your own mental barriers—the negative voices in your head that make up your personal "pirates" and that truly thrive on taking over your ship. In other words, you need to get out of your own way.

That's not to say you will succeed without a plan, without support, and without making decisions that are well thought out and intentional. There's a lot that goes into living your dreams, and that's where the reality sets in. But make no mistake about it: The reality has no place inside your dreams. The reality only comes into the planning stage.

My experience has taught me that the concepts outlined in this book are not solely for a literal cutting of your bowlines, but for any figurative cutting and setting out on a course about which you've been dreaming and to which you've been aspiring. These principles can be applied to any goal or any leap you want to make, whether it's a project you've wanted to take on, travel on which you've been wanting to embark, a career change you've been wanting to make, or an experience you've been seeking.

If you have a dream or have been wanting at your very core to do something, but you've been saying to yourself that it's not realistic, you're too old or too young, you're not qualified or don't have the experience, or you don't have the money or the ability, think again.

My hope is that this book will provide you with the tools necessary to create a mind shift for you to take your own leap, sail off into the sunset, or do whatever it is that you've always dreamed of doing.

Here's what I know to be true: The starting point is the dream. Everything else is simply the plan. And your plan can begin right here, by leaping first into this book.

To young men contemplating a voyage,
I would say go.

-Joshua Slocum (1844-1909):
First solo circumnavigator, bestselling author

FINDINGS, FAST FACTS, AND FIRST PHOTOS

Polynesian women really do wear flowers in their hair. Really. It's not just a touristy thing. In fact, there is little touristy about the island of Nuku Hiva in the Marquesan Islands of French Polynesia. It's also rather refreshing that there is little American about it. The cruising community here, as expected, is much more international. No, Barbara, you're not in Mexico anymore.

The Great and Mysterious Polynesian Migration is believed to have occurred somewhere around 3,500 years ago when the first settlers left Southeast Asia, Taiwan, or China in sailing/paddling canoes (the forerunners to our lovely catamaran) with chickens, dogs, pigs, veggies, and their kids. They used celestial navigation and read cloud reflections, bird flight patterns, and wave formations (ancient techniques long lost) to arrive who-knows-how-many-days-or-months-later to the western islands of Samoa and Tonga.

...

The French claimed what is now French Polynesia (made up of the Marquesas Islands, the Tuamotu Archipelago, and the Society Islands, including Tahiti, Bora Bora, and

Huahine) in 1838. While European settlement all but decimated the Polynesian culture with disease, alcohol, firearms, and evangelism, there has been a resurgence of national pride since the 1980's ...

The people are lovely. As we walk through the streets, they will stop to ask about where we come from and will readily tell us about their lives here. Almost everyone (men, women, and teens) is tattooed, an ancient Polynesian art that was adopted by sailors when Captain James Cook first arrived in French Polynesia in the late 1700's ... The artwork is spectacular.

I am loving speaking French. And I'm really speaking French, none of the tongue-tied stuff I attempt whenever I travel to Quebec. I've surprised my entire family with my skill, but not more than I've surprised myself. I haven't been in French conversations for nearly 35 years. And I'm doing my fair share as I act as the translator for most of our cruising friends here.

We have had to get over sticker shock since we've been here. There are only a handful of restaurants, which are very pricey. We did sample the local specialty of "poisson cru," which is raw fish marinated in lime juice and coconut milk – amazing, even if it was served without a vegetable. This should have been a foreshadow for us: While fruit is abundant on the island, vegetables are a bit more scarce.

That doesn't affect the cost of produce either way, however. We spent about US$50 on a mere few pieces of produce when we first arrived, and have supplemented here and there with other very expensive pieces of fruit and vegetable. The various "magasins" (stores) are well stocked with canned goods, however, including "haricots verts" (green beans) that I so desperately but unsuccessfully sought in Puerto Vallarta. Any items in the store with a red price label are subsidized by the French government, which apparently pours millions in to these islands ...

One way around the prices for fresh produce is to pick it yourself, which we've gotten really good at. There isn't much choice in the way of vegetables (although we've seen avocadoes growing – only too high or far for our reach). We've had incredible pamplemousse (grapefruit), starfruit, mangoes, papayas, bananas, and guavas, many right off the trees. We call it foraging. Simply luscious.

This place is pure paradise. No dangerous life-threatening animals to fear (other than sharks in the water – a story unto itself)—even the dogs take it slow. Lush green steep mountains rising up from the sea. Fertile volcanic soil. More fruit trees than one can imagine. Beautiful people. Beautiful singing. Beautiful dances (we were lucky enough to watch a practice one night passing the community center). It truly must have been the ideal life before the white man turned things around – although it is still pretty incredible.

It does rain a lot here, usually only for a few moments and usually only a few times a day, but we have gotten used to the drill. Close or vent all hatches whenever we leave the boat, even if it's clear sunshine. Sleep with hatches vented. If drying anything out, be ready to take it all in when it starts to rain, and then take it back out to finish drying – and then multiply this by a few times. We're also trying to dry out our heavy comforters and decorative pillows, so that we can store them in vacuum sealed bags. We're hoping to achieve this before mold sets in, which is a huge *problem here, and this has proven to be a multi-day task, as well.*

We've been a bit relieved with the mostly overcast skies, given the alternative hot and humid sunshine. Because it's been so hot, we've been getting up with the sunrise around 6 a.m. or before, so that our boat projects and school are done by noon. The Saturday market begins at 4 or 5 (we're still not sure) – we got there at 5:30 a.m.—but we do know that all the good produce was gone by 6:08 a.m.

It took us a good five days to finally melt into normal sleeping patterns. We've been spending our days on boat projects, school, and exploring the island with a couple of hikes under our belts and some visits to some archeological sites. We've now had all three of our sails repaired—while the mainsail was the major job to have the headboard re-attached, we also had some tears in both our jib and our screecher. The sail repair here was well done, and at fairly reasonable prices, too. So far, so good.

...

Our days are full, and we are feeling very content.

-Barb
Taiohae Bay, Nuku Hiva, Marquesas Islands, French Polynesia

LESSON 1:

Throwing Off Your Bowlines: Get Started

The person who goes farthest is generally the one who is willing to do and dare. The sure-thing boat never gets far from shore.

-Dale Carnegie (1888-1955)
Bestselling author, lecturer

It is part of the human condition to want to feel that we matter in this world. What makes us feel like we matter is when we are living in line with who we are and who we were meant to be. Although many of us cannot articulate our life purpose, it is there and with some coaxing can be revealed. Either way, each one of us is a unique being, with unique talents so core to who we are that sometimes we don't even know that what we do is special and unique. We've been living with it so long that it's like the tip of our noses—because we don't notice it, we take it for granted. When we are seen for this specialness, we feel acknowledged and recognized for who we *really* are. We feel seen. We feel truly alive.

On the contrary, when we are not living according to who we really are, we feel dissonant, bored, aggravated, and misaligned.

Our dreams and aspirations—what we've always wanted to do but haven't yet achieved—are where our ultimate aliveness and resonance lives. Resonance describes the feeling of certainty we get in our gut that tells us we are doing the right thing, or are where we need to be, or the choice we are making is absolutely the right one.

Personal growth happens when we make changes, but only when the change comes from within, from that place of resonance. When we maintain the status quo, we get stale and live in a state of dissonance—that place of "there's got to be more." In other words, change for the sake of change or one that has been imposed upon us may not get us to a state of resonance, but change that is aligned with who we are, whether big or small, keeps us fresh.

For many, making change feels uncomfortable. No matter, life does begin at the edge of your comfort zone.

While change is where personal growth happens, we also need it to keep us moving forward. Forward movement brings fulfillment and, in turn, allows us to move closer to achieving what we aspire to achieve. The movement forward could begin with little things, like starting an exercise class or saying "no" to something we've always said "yes" to. Momentum can get you to make bigger changes—like sailing with your family for two-and-a-half years.

Regardless of the size of the change, moving toward our dreams allows us to grow, and we begin to feel like we are heading closer toward who we were meant to be. When we are living as we were meant to live, we realize the impact we were meant to be making in this world and contribute in a way we were meant to contribute.

Think about it: When was the last time you made a change that resonated with you? I'm willing to bet that you felt accomplished, and as a result, inspired, and with that, you were able to walk a bit taller.

There's a sense of accomplishment in making changes that you choose for yourself. The freshness and growth that comes along with it keeps you inspired. When inspired, you can be so much more able to live in line with who you are and who you were meant to be. Inspiration is the best motivator to propel you forward toward things you otherwise wouldn't believe you could do—in other words, achieving your dream, creating the impact you want to have, and feeling so fully alive. All you need is to get started, and the momentum will continue to carry you forward as you continue to work on maintaining that momentum.

But I've already achieved a lot in my life and people around me already see me as successful. Why do I still feel that there's got to be more to life?

Through my work and life experiences, I've come across many high achievers who seem to be full of forward momentum. They've gone to college, had successful careers, built businesses, had families, and made a lot of money. According to the society that they live in, they look "successful." The truth for them, however, is they followed a path they thought they *should* be following and have stopped becoming conscious about what they really want. After a while, they start asking, "Isn't there more to all this?"

Many of us go down the path of life making decisions and choices based on what we think we should be doing, but not necessarily resonant in our fullest selves. In other words, the choices we make may be aligned with our need for accomplishment and success, but are not as aligned with our passions. Ultimately, sooner or later, we wake up and realize this. It's unavoidable. We need to feel more fully alive, or we feel that we are starting to wither.

While I was coaching the CEO of a large technology company, he reflected that, although his successes seemed impressive, "truly if I died tomorrow, I don't feel like I've accomplished what I was meant to do, or that I've had an impact that is meaningful to me, or that I've left a legacy worth leaving. And meanwhile, I feel life's clock ticking away."

It's what I call the Big Deal Syndrome. For some, contributing to the technology industry, with its innovation and fast pace, might be the passion and legacy that my client was looking for, but everyone is different. Each individual must ask him or herself: If I were to die tomorrow, am I satisfied with the impact I've had? Do the things I've done fit in with my passions and dreams? Have I begun to create a legacy that I am proud of?

If the answer is no, it's time to make a change. It's time to go after those passions and dreams. Tomorrow will come no matter what you do, whether you go after your dreams or not. You might as well be spending the time effectively working toward doing what you were meant to be doing. The alternative is to wake up tomorrow suffering from the same Big Deal Syndrome you are living today. And one day, you won't wake up at all.

There's a natural synergy to having everyone follow their passion. If everyone does whatever it is that they were meant to be doing—whether it is being a talented artist who creates beauty for the world, a passionate bridge builder who skillfully designs for efficient transportation, or a person in technology who is passionate about innovation and being on the cusp of what's new in the world—life for all falls into place. This natural synergy creates healthier communities and, ultimately, a healthier world. So you see, it's not just about you and me. It's far, far bigger than that.

What if I don't have a dream or a passion?

According to a survey I conducted about creating successful change, over one-quarter of the respondents did not have a big goal, dream, or passion, even though they wanted one.

Regardless of your spiritual leanings or whether you have any at all, everyone has unique gifts that are the result of their unique combination of their traits, personality, skills, passions, and interests. These strengths, or gifts, are so innate to who you are that you may not have realized that you have them. And it's key to understand that many of these gifts are not necessarily a "doing" thing, but rather a "being" thing— who you are as you show up in the world.

I took a class some years ago in which I crafted my own Life Purpose Statement to help me define my life's mission. I came up with the following: "To help people live happy and healthy lives so they feel inspired to follow their dreams." As I read it to my fellow classmates, I said, "This is a bit silly. It sounds like a greeting card. That's how I sign my greeting cards. Don't you all sign your greeting cards like this?" The response I got was blank stares. And that's when I had an "aha" moment: Not everyone thinks this way; this isn't everyone's mission. I realized then that was one of the unique things about me because that's where my natural inclinations lie—to help people feel good about themselves so they can then go out and live their dreams.

In my work, I've come across people who are very clear about their dreams and how those dreams fit in with their unique calling. Others really don't know their calling at all, and still others seem to be on the right path without even knowing it, but aren't aware of where they're headed notwithstanding they are going in the right direction. For these last two groups, the choices they have made thus far in life have no context for them and, therefore, they feel disempowered.

Knowing your life purpose contextualizes the decisions you make in your life. When you are faced with a choice, and you know what you were meant to be doing, you will know whether your choice is in alignment with who you are. In other words, knowing your life purpose acts as a beacon for your life. It's really as simple as that.

For those who feel they don't have a passion, I believe they just haven't found it yet. Everyone has a calling, a passion, a dream, and it's only a matter of drawing it out for yourself.

Exercises have been provided at the end of this chapter to help you discover your dreams and passions. Knowing where you're headed is the first step to creating a life with meaning, the impact you were meant to have, and the legacy you were meant to be leaving.

Why is getting started so difficult?

Imagine yourself sailing along a river. The wind is in your hair, the sun is shining, and it's an absolutely perfect day. Suddenly, up ahead you see a massive boulder in the water. The waters around the boulder get angrier and faster. You have the choice of heading to the safety of shore or of navigating your way around the boulder. As you get closer, it seems like the boulder gets bigger and bigger, and you switch your focus between the safety of shore and this looming boulder. You know that if you choose the shore, you'll put an end to the day without reaching your destination. If you stay the course, you'll soon catch the boulder out of the corner of your eye as you pass by it. And then it's behind you. And you go on to the next one, which doesn't feel as difficult to navigate because you've seen that you've gotten past it before and can do it again. In this way, you'll reach your destination.

Managing your way around change is like learning any life skill—practice makes it easier. If you are someone who regularly takes risks, goes out of your comfort zone, and is conscious about personal growth, then the next change is not as difficult as for someone who lives a "routine" life. Becoming proficient at taking leaps requires making changes along the way.

As an aside, if you haven't made a change in a long time, there is still hope to get on your path. Start with making a small change that feels resonant for you—something that you've been wanting to do. Whatever you do, though, do keep the momentum going so you'll have more confidence to make the next change.

Even more important than being used to making change, the key to what makes it so difficult is this: It's those voices in our heads, the negative self talk, the "pirates" that invade our minds and keep us from reaching our most important successes. They tell you: "You're going to crash into that boulder," "You don't know how to sail this thing," "Who are you to think you can get around that boulder?" These pirates are trying to get you to maintain the status quo, to thwart your efforts to go where you want to go, to take the easy way out, and, in effect, to protect you from making a mistake. They have been with you since you were able to start judging yourself and will be with you until the day you die. And as you get closer to that boulder, in essence to making an important change, those pirates get louder and louder. But here's the thing:

The key to achieving your dreams is how you navigate your pirates. How you deal with your pirates is what will determine whether or not you can take the necessary steps to follow your dreams.

Any important change will be accompanied by those pirates. Expect it and be prepared.

How do I know if it's my pirates holding me back or my inner truth telling me I'm on the wrong path?

The difference between your pirates holding you back and your own inner truth telling you that you are not on the right path lies in the level of resonance you have for the path that you are on.

The waters of the South Pacific are warm and inviting. They sparkle the kind of blue-green seen only in postcards, are abundant with plant and sea life, and have incredible visibility sometimes 60-feet deep. What better way to experience this spectacle than by snorkeling. I love snorkeling—although only in warm water—and it's one of the most fulfilling things I could possibly do. However, in the South Pacific, if you are going to snorkel, you have to be prepared to encounter sharks. Every. Single. Time. I was scared to death, even though I knew that others before me were able to do it safely, and if I was to fully experience life in the South Pacific, I had to come to terms with this. Notwithstanding my fears, swimming and encountering sharks safely was so resonant for me that it took my breath away, even as I literally took the leap, each and every time, into the water. I just knew that I had to get past my pirates.

Thursday,
May 19, 2011

A WORD ON SHARKS

It's been a real treat to swim in the crystal clear white-sand-bottom, coral-lined bay of Anaho, a picturesque paradise on the north side of Nuku Hiva. And the treat is not just the eye candy. We've been unable (or unwilling) to do any extensive swimming in Taiohae Bay, a black sand bay, known to be home to plenty of sharks and where we spent our first 13 days after making landfall. Rumor has it that a local boy was bitten by a shark last year and died of his wounds. Tempting fate is not on my "to do" list.

However, as our friend and former Danish navy diver said when warned of the sharks by another cruiser while he was diving our anchor, sharks are everywhere in the ocean – especially in tropical waters. This happens to be particularly true in the South Pacific, where apparently a ridiculously large percentage of the world's shark population lives. The fact is if we want to truly experience the South Pacific, we have to get comfortable swimming in the water.

Here is what our friend Caren (who cruised with her family for five years) said about overcoming our fear of swimming with sharks:

1. *Get a good shark book (we have one). Knowledge is power over our fears, so get to know the different kinds of sharks, which are the aggressive ones, and what their different behavior means. They show curiosity first, so there is plenty of time to get out of the water before they start showing agitation, arching, or circling behavior, which precedes an attack. Apparently, most of the sharks we will see on our trip will be reef sharks, both black and white tip, which are used to eating small reef fish. This means that we are not their natural food, so they may come to check us out, but then they move on...*

2. *Ask the locals. Caren warns that other cruisers are often ignorant about sharks and give misinformation based on their fears and inexperience. So in addition to learning from a reliable written or online source, it makes sense that the locals are a great source of knowledge about the sharks in their particular area. They'll know if any tiger sharks have been around, for example, and if so, it's important to stay clear. Simply do as the locals do...*

3. *Be prepared. Have a Hawaiian slingshot handy while swimming in water with many sharks, although Caren and her family never actually had the need to use one. Hawaiian sling shots are used for spear fishing, and they look like a long rod with a few sharp metal pokes at the end. Caren suggested finding them in Mexican fishing stores, but here we are already in the South Pacific without any. We'll have to do without.*

4. *Be calm when you see a shark. It's important to remember that we are not their normal food, so they don't automatically think of us as food. They do, however, have an uncanny ability to sense fear and distress. Their normal prey are the weak and injured creatures, so if you splash and scream and act like you are in trouble, you look an awful lot like a weak and injured creature. Stay calm, and they just figure you are some other big fish ...*

5. *Get over it. Overcoming our fear of sharks, any way we can, will ensure that we can fully experience their mystery and beauty. We are fortunate to have sharks still roaming the waters of the South Pacific, since most cruising grounds in*

the Atlantic are devoid of these creatures due to overfishing. Caren encourages us to snorkel at the passes, or entrances, to the atolls in the Tuamotus, well known for shark hangouts. For example, there are all kinds of sharks breeding at the atoll entrance at Rangiroa, where the water is known to resemble a shark screensaver because there are so many sharks. People come from all over the world to dive this pass. And our guide book tells us there are many more like it, which can be experienced by scuba diving or just plain snorkeling while at a slack or incoming tide (called drift diving/ snorkeling).

6. *Know the statistics: The statistics are much worse on the highway, and we never hesitate to drive, so, Caren says, don't let fear of sharks ruin your experience of some of the best underwater spots on earth. She assures us that we would be missing half the trip if we don't go in the water.*

We'll keep you posted on any face to face encounters, but since there haven't been any yet, we don't have any photos for you. In addition, our Internet is way too slow to start looking for them online. For now, though, we're studying up from our shark book.

-Barb in Anaho Bay, Nuku Hiva, Marquesas

When something is exciting for me, I know it because it takes my breath away. Even though it scares me so badly that it feels like I'm choking, I want to do it anyway. And if I can imagine myself having achieved that exciting thing and I still feel empowered and excited about it, I know that it's my pirates telling me not to do it. That's my place of resonance: I do need to get prepared for what I'm about to face, but I need to do whatever it is that scares me, anyway.

What if I make a change and it wasn't the right one?

One of my dear cruising friends worried that her dream to cross the Pacific and cruise the South Pacific was developed in her twenties. Now she was in her mid-forties. How was she to know if it still mattered? What if she got there and it wasn't what she had thought it would be?

You know it's still the right dream if you are still excited about the prospect of achieving success on that dream. The What Ifs are your pirates, without a doubt. And if you don't go after your dream, then you'll never confirm that, in fact, you can do it, or worse yet, you'll continue living with your Big Deal Syndrome.

Many of us also suffer from Analysis Paralysis, the syndrome of being so afraid of making the wrong choice that we don't even begin to act. Taking the first step needs to happen if you are to move forward, however. There is always room for change. If you find as you go along that it is not right, then you must realign. You have the choice to make it right again by making a different change or adjusting the one you are already making. A wise person (my older sister) once told me that it really does all work out in the end, and if it's not working out yet, then it's not the end: We can always re-route ourselves, and we have the power to make the choices necessary to do that.

On day 15 of our 20-day Pacific crossing, the reinforced webbing at the top of the mainsail came undone, detached from the sail, and caused the entire mainsail to fall to the deck. The halyard (the rope that attaches to the top of the sail and is used to haul up the sail) was at the top of the mast. This meant that even if we could repair the sail en route, we had no way of hauling it back to the top of the mast. One option was to get the halyard down by climbing to the top of the mast. For me, the danger of this option—being out at sea in big swells, which would make the climber swing like a pendulum— was too dangerous. The only other option was to do nothing, as far as we could tell. Yet not having a main sail is pretty serious. We were close to a week from landfall, with only four days of fuel remaining in our tanks, and no mainsail.

Out at sea, giving up is not an option. Since it wasn't yet working out, we knew it wasn't yet the end of the line. What had us keep moving was the belief that this situation would work out, one way or another. And it did. We kept at it, used our much smaller foresail, and made landfall safely five days later (where, incidentally, we were able to get our mainsail repaired, climb to the top of the mast to get the halyard back, and re-rig the boat for our next passage).

Life is like any sailing voyage. It's not a dress rehearsal. You get one chance to make the crossing. Giving up cannot be an option. You need to keep going, moving forward, keeping that momentum, until you get there.

Getting started is the first step to getting that momentum. Once you begin to move forward, your perspective changes and things become apparent to you that were not apparent from where you stood before you started moving. The right routing will become apparent only as you go.

Several years ago, I worked with a client whose dream was to buy an island somewhere in the tropics and create an ecotourist destination. While she wasn't prepared to start working toward it while she still had children at home, she kept the idea at the back of her mind. Just by identifying what she was wanting got her started, and although the momentum slowed down slightly, she was able to keep her eyes and ears open. Years later, I met up with her and the first thing she said to me was: "I bought a children's bookstore—and that's my island!"

Some people know very specifically what they want to do, and some don't. Our dreams, however, are wound up in who we are as beings, and our dreams enliven us because of what they bring to us, not necessarily because of what we are doing. As long as we come to the state of being that we are wanting from any particular dream, it will keep us enlivened and passionate. In other words, what we end up with might not actually come about by doing what we set out to do. It is, ultimately, a way of being, or how we show up in the world, that we all seek.

Once you get started, you will become aware of things you need to know or do that weren't apparent from the starting line. Your perspective changes as you move forward, both physically and mentally.

My own personal story of how I came to my life coaching career is illustrative of how forward movement got me to where I needed to go, notwithstanding I changed my perspective on how to get where I wanted to go. When I was heading to college and needed to declare a major, my consciousness told me that I should go into psychology, but for various reasons, I ended up in law school. After ten years of practicing law and some other career fits and starts, I finally gave in to my deep truth that, "I love helping people feel good about themselves when they are not starting out that way, so they can then go out into the world to be the best they can be." That was how I wanted to show up in the world since it really was an extension of who I am. My belief was that the only way to get there was through being a psychologist. I began researching psychology programs, while still being adamant that I was not willing to spend another eight to ten years re-training. In the process of doing my research, I came across life coaching and realized that's what I had been describing in my dream career all along. I had no idea when I set out that that's where I would be.

Don't let your pirates get the better of you. Don't let them stop you from even getting started and making a move. Choose a path, any path, and start moving. You can adjust your course as you go. But if you don't even leave the dock, you are certain not to go anywhere.

What if I don't succeed at making this change?

One out of four respondents to my survey about making successful change indicated that the fear of failure has stopped them from moving forward toward their goal.

One of the scariest things for high achievers is to go after what we really want, for the very reason that we *are* high achievers. We consider ourselves to be people who succeed—at a lot of things. As high achievers, what if we are not successful at something we actually love and are passionate about?! That would be the scariest thing of all.

On the other hand, how will you ever know? It's as simple as this: Just get moving. National Hockey League superstar Wayne Gretzky once said, "You will miss 100 percent of the shots that you never take." If you don't even try, you're certain not to succeed.

I've heard it said that every boat in the South Pacific has come in contact with a reef at least once, but there are two types of sailors: Those who admit to it, and those don't. A "mistake" must not be viewed as a failure, but rather as the weather patterns that are letting you know that you should change your course. No one gets to success without re-routing. After all, if it's not yet working out, it's because you are not yet finished with your task.

If I go after my dreams now and actually succeed, I'm worried that there won't be anything left after I'm done.

Many successful people don't even begin the route that they really want to be taking for fear that there will be nothing left after they've gotten there. They worry that life will be completely devoid of excitement, so why not simply live with some minor aliveness now, which they know, than end up with a huge high from making it to their destination and then a major dip on the excitement and aliveness scale when there's nothing as good that follows.

I can promise you this: There will always be more, and that's what's remarkable about being human. Once you've achieved what you really want, you are so excited about life that you'll keep going and find more. You'll be even better equipped the next time around with more confidence that you can indeed get past your pirates with greater ease.

There's no such thing as having nothing left, until, of course, you die. That's not to say you won't have to work for your "Next Big Thing," but anything worthwhile requires work. The bottom line is that there's no time like the present. If you don't work toward getting what you really want now, the time may never come. Do it now.

How do I know what I was meant to be doing?

One of the things to remember when examining your dreams is not to censor yourself. There is no reality in the dream—that's why it's called a dream. On the other hand, reality comes into play during the planning stage only.

If you would have told me the day before my husband suggested his sailing dream that it was possible for me to experience firsthand my own travel dream, I would have told you that you were crazy. The dream *was* crazy—in fact, so much so that I hadn't actually allowed myself to think about it. What I needed to realize was that even though it felt like a crazy dream in my mind, that didn't matter. In order to turn a dream into reality, you must focus on logistics. I can do logistics. We can all do logistics.

In figuring out what one of my clients was meant to be doing, where she fit into this world, and what impact she was meant to have, she stated that she dreamed of being just like Christiane Amanpour, the CNN correspondent who reports from war zones. After sheepishly admitting to this dream, she said: "This is crazy. I am forty-something, have two kids and a husband, and there's no way I'm going to do that." Perhaps not, and that's a choice she's made and continues to make, but there can be some reconciliation with what she would get out of being Christiane Amanpour that she can look for elsewhere. In our analysis, she felt thrilled by being at the forefront of heated issues that are current and widespread, of being seen as an expert in these issues, and of high visibility. Other options she could consider and which she felt resonant included involvement in creating documentaries, exploring journalism (writing or broadcasting), getting involved in local issues, reporting about them, or advising different constituents affected by them, going back to school and studying international issues that were compelling for her so she could become the expert and ultimately to advise government. Some of these options could take upwards of ten years, but ten years was going to come no matter what, so she might as well be working toward being in that place she's dreaming. Then, come ten years, she'll be living her dreams and not still dreaming about them.

Tuesday, December 7, 2010

ON GAS AND WIND

I'm on sunrise duty again. We're more than halfway to Zihuatenajo and hope to make it in by tomorrow morning. We've been motoring for over 24 hours now as the winds are very light or non-existent and coming from directly behind us. That's the problem with Mexico cruising. Either there's a weather warning, where we stay put, or there's a weather window, which means there's no wind.

Michael and I had a familiar conversation at 1:30 a.m. this morning, except it usually takes place in a car on a road trip somewhere: Should we stop and get gas?

Although we started this passage with a full tank (105 gallons), our fuel gauge seems only to work intermittently. Most of the time it shows we are completely full. So Michael (aka MacGyver) has taken to measuring the gas in the tank by using a long wooden dowel and then measuring the fuel level with a ruler. We keep track of our engine hours, so this way we can figure out how much fuel we use per hour. Based on our estimates, we'll barely make it to Zihuatenajo, unless we get some real sailing in later today. That's what I'm hoping for.

Usually, in a car, like many men I know, Michael's the one to "risk" it, which drives me crazy as I'm always worried we'll run out of gas and get stranded somewhere. I like the security of a full tank of gas (and, as an aside, a clean boat—another oddity of mine: I must start a passage with a clean boat—I was up 'til all hours the night before we left cleaning the windows ...).

This time, I'm willing to risk it, even if it means we have to bob around for a while, going reeeeaaaaallllly slowwwwwly, using only our sails. And, of course, cars don't have the option of hoisting a sail.

Like this longer 3 to 4 day passage, I figure it's a good dress rehearsal if we do end up going to the South Pacific, which we still haven't decided on yet. You see, this lack of wind requiring us to motor most of the time would continue into Central America. In the meantime, if we go to the South Pacific, there is much more wind. On the other hand, based on our calculations, we'd be spending 25% of our days getting to and around the South Pacific being on a passage (including 3+ weeks at sea just getting there, without seeing any land, or having the option of seeing any land, for that matter). But at least we'd be sailing, even if some of it is merely bobbing. With the continuous hum of the motor giving me a headache all day yesterday and continuing into today, the South Pacific is sounding much more attractive.

Sun is rising, dolphins at our bow. It's not all bad.

-Barb, 12 miles offshore, approx. 20 miles south of Manzanillo (we didn't stop for gas) 18 degrees 41.611 minutes North by 104 degrees 10.372 minutes West

P.S. Now that we've passed Manzanillo, we are officially the furthest south we've been yet. Another milestone.

Here's what I know to be true: I grew exponentially from this leap into adventure, in ways I never dreamed of. The difficult part was simply making the leap. That's all I needed to get me started on my path.

Not all who wander are lost.

-JRR Tolkien (1892-1973)
English writer, poet, professor

EXERCISE:
Discovering Your Dreams

For many, the key to figuring out how to live on purpose and follow your dreams is to ask yourself the ten questions listed below. Not every question may speak to you, but if you haven't yet identified your dream, or you don't know the impact you want to have, or the legacy you want to leave, there should be at least a few questions listed that can help you get started on your path toward that leap, to move you closer to whatever you were meant to do and be in your lifetime.

1. What are you passionate about? What are the issues and causes that draw you in or that you care deeply about?

2. Where do you "go" when confronted with other people's issues or problems? What are your natural inclinations? For example, are you the fixer, the resourceful one, the nurturer, the relationship broker, the leader, the cheerleader?

3. Who are you when you are feeling at your best? Ask the people who are close to you. Think about what adults said about you as a child. Think about who you are now to your friends, family, and/or colleagues. What can they count on you for, almost every time they encounter you?

4. If you could do anything you wanted, without the possibility of failure, without any fears, and with the full support, faith, and encouragement of everyone around you, what would it be?

5. If you can change jobs with anyone on this planet, who would it be and why?

6. If your face appeared on the cover of any magazine, which magazine would you want it to be? What would you want the cover story to be about?

7. If you had $1.5 million to invest in three ventures ($500,000 each), each one guaranteed to succeed, what ventures would they be? These could be businesses, organizations, start-ups, grants, personal hobbies, i.e., anything.

8. Imagine yourself ten years from now, being called onto a stage to receive an honor. What would the honor be for? What would people be saying about you as they introduced you?

9. If your cell phone was to ring and it was you, 20 years from now having accomplished your dreams, what would your older self tell you about the next 20 years?

10. What have you always dreamed of doing?

RARO FRIENDS

They say that people and not places make good memories, and our time in Rarotonga, Cook Islands is no exception.

First we met Ron McKenzie, who did some mechanical work on our engine and generously opened his home to us and introduced us to his family. Ron is from Australia but has lived in Rarotonga for nearly 25 years now. Michael spent a day at his home catching up on the Internet, and they generously gifted us dozens of passion fruit and pawpaw (local speak for papaya).

We rented scooters one day to tour the island, the highlight of which was stopping into the Maire Nui Gardens, an oasis of seven acres of spectacular tropical gardens in Titikaveka on the southeast corner of the island. There met Hinano and John, who run the gardens and the cafe (where we had dinner one night—incredible food with the world's greatest cheesecake—lemon meringue—and not to be missed!). Hinano and John became our hosts for the remainder of our stay, loaning us their truck, and allowing us use of their home for beachfront access for a day of relaxing by the sea (the *most spectacular beach on the island with amazing coral to snorkel—they rent out a home/haven right next door: check out heliconiahideaway.com).*

The two of them are fascinating people. John breeds race horses and owns a winery back in his native Australia. He met Hinano 30 years ago on a visit to the island, and then came back 8 years ago when he married her (I'm always a sucker for great love stories!). Hinano is the 16th generation descendant of the original Cook Islands natives, the coming together of Samoan and Marquesan royal families who decided to rule the island together to maintain peace. Today, the "ariki" or chiefs of the ruling families still maintain power and act as advisors to the elected government. The chiefdoms continue to be handed down to the firstborn, whether male or female. Hinano's grandmother was the Big Chief, so to speak, and lived in the palace, which Hinano allowed us to tour. The palace is an unpretentious large two-story home with a wraparound porch surrounded by acres of gorgeous land, a marae (ancient ceremonial grounds) in the back, and a cemetery, where we visited her grandparents' graves. The palace is private property, but while the house is locked up now, we visited the grounds, got to peek in the windows and see all the furniture. It looks like it has been closed up for many years ... We were fascinated to learn firsthand about the culture and politics of the Cook Islands from Hinano and John and marveled at the fact that we have become friends with real live royalty! Besides, they are great people, and we spent some great times with them. They surprised Michael and me for our birthdays when they brought their famous cheesecake as the birthday cake for our potluck dinner to share with our friends aboard Britannia and Piko, and with Ron, his wife, Gina, and their daughter, Rongina.

Two additional interesting facts about Raro: Landholding is handed down by families, which may account for the fact that there is no real poverty on the island. And families bury their loved ones right on their property—a comforting thought to have your loved ones, even dead loved ones, close by.

-Barb
Docked at Avatiu Harbor, Rarotonga, Cook Islands

LESSON 2:

Weathering the Storm Within:
The True Reason Why We Don't Go After
What We Really Want

---

*There is nothing more enticing, disenchanting,
and enslaving than the life at sea.*

-Joseph Conrad (1857-1924)
Polish/British author

If our dreams are so compelling, and we've thought about them or kept them at the back of our consciousness for so long, why is it that so few of us actually go after them? Why don't we go after what we really, really want, not after the "success" that others impose upon us? In one word: Pirates.

Our personal pirates are those parts of us that are rather subversive, that whisper in our brains so subtly that we think they are part of our personal truth, those saboteurs of exciting compelling plans. Our pirates seem to attack our psyche just as we approach doing something that takes our breath away, and they work harder and harder to sabotage our efforts as we get closer and closer to taking the leap.

In my life and work experience, there is no question that the single most important factor that keeps successful people from choosing to go after what they really want and instead choosing to go after the "safe" success is how they navigate their pirates. The problem begins when people don't pay attention to their pirates, because it sounds counter-intuitive to do so. We've been taught for so long not to listen to the negativity, but when we don't listen to it, we tend to accept it as part of our real selves. Subconsciously, we take what our pirates say and incorporate it as truth. The result: Our pirates separate us from being our truest, highest, and best selves.

It's not that successful people who actually follow their dreams don't have their own personal pirates. Nor is it that they've learned to rid themselves of all their pirates. Believe it or not, they have their own pirates, very similar to yours. The difference is that they've learned to navigate them.

You will never rid yourself of your pirates. Somehow they've latched onto you from early in your intellectual and emotional development and have been keeping you in check since then. Some of us have been better at keeping them at bay than others. Still, some of us have allowed them to grow, to get louder and more boisterous to the point that it's hard to believe that there's any other way to live.

Your pirates are extremely adept at helping you maintain your status quo by convincing you "That's just the way it is." If that's what you are hearing, it is your first clue that your pirates are very present.

What are the mantras voiced by our pirates to maintain the status quo and keep us from making important changes?

Our pirates' excuses are packaged up in so many different mantras, but all can generally fit within one of the following five categories:

1. That's just the way it is, or that's just the way it's done. As in: You're stuck here. There's a real sense of struggle and sacrifice in this mantra. It's full of martyrdom. It makes you a victim of your circumstances. And it's saying: Who are you to think that things could be different? You're not special. Nor are you lucky, like all the really successful people who actually live their dreams.

2. You don't have enough. As in: You don't have enough time for this, especially not now. You don't have the resources, the knowledge, the wherewithal, the money, the support. While the successful people have all those things, it's unrealistic to think you'll ever get them.

3. You're not enough. As in: You're not smart enough (or as smart as all those other successful people are). You're not good enough to do this. You especially are not entitled to this. What have you done to deserve this? You are simply not worthy enough and besides, you're already not successful enough. Who are you to think anyone will listen to you? Or go along with you?

4. You shouldn't. As in: You are so selfish for wanting this. Your family (or your boss, the organization, or someone or something else) needs you, and you'd be

letting them down. They are relying on you, and you are a terrible person for abandoning them.

5. Your dream is just too insignificant to matter. As in: There are far greater issues facing this planet (like starving kids in Africa). Who are you to think your dream is important? You are so self-absorbed for wanting such a ridiculous thing.

I am willing to bet that one of those pirate voices shows up in your head to insist that you have no right to make a change. It keeps us in the status-quo, and therefore, to a certain extent, our pirates protect us—from failure and discomfort. While it keeps us comfortable, however, it tricks us into thinking that we should not or could not do what we really want to do.

Your pirates will be with you for the rest of your life. Whatever they are saying to you, they are, indeed, saving you from failure. But at the same time, they are also "saving" you from living your life as you were meant to be living it.

What if I really and truly don't have enough time, money, or resources to do what I want to do? Isn't that a good enough reason not to do it?

The results of my survey about making successful change indicated that 35% of the respondents believe that they do not have the time or resources to go after what they really want.

We may not articulate the true pirate voices we hear, but they manifest themselves in other ways. We say that we don't have the time, the money, or the resources. The reality is, however, that these are deeply entrenched pirates. By acknowledging that we do, indeed, have pirates, we can understand that the excuses are really just logistical hurdles that we are hiding behind. If we were to get to that "Whatever it Takes" point when we no longer contemplate "Should I do this?," but rather get to the planning stage of "How do I get there?," we'd find the time, the money, and the resources.

One of my clients was a stay-at-home mom, who, together with her husband, determined that her role would be primary caregiver and taking care of the household while her children were young. Up until this time, she hadn't found anything that inspired her enough to go outside the parameters of her role, so when her husband, a corporate executive, had business commitments or travelled, her schedule would bend to accommodate his obligations. In the meantime, she knew there was something out there that fulfilled her purpose in life beyond her family, but was not yet clear on what it was.

After working together, she came to the realization that her place in the world was to work on a particular political issue and educate people about it. When she spoke of the issue, it visibly moved her. In connecting with this passion, she came to that "Whatever it Takes" place, where she decided: "I must do this. I cannot sit back any longer. I must take steps to have an impact on this issue."

When she did decide to commit to living her dream, something shifted in her. She researched programs to learn more about the issue. In doing so, she came across one that excited her, but was an hour's drive away and required her to attend in person one day every month, leaving early in the morning and coming home late at night. This required her to make arrangements for childcare coverage—getting the kids to school, having them picked up after school, having them looked after between the time school let out and when her husband came home, and have dinner arranged for her family. When she examined it, it was no longer about the time or her other obligations. It now was about logistics. And guess what? She managed. She made all the arrangements necessary to attend this program for the year. As a result, she became more alive, more excited, a better parent, and a better wife. When it's important enough, you realize that your barriers become logistical—and then very clearly surmountable.

Remember when my husband dropped the bombshell on me that we should rent out the house, buy a boat, and go cruising? My initial reaction was far from allowing it to happen. I told him I didn't know how to sail, I don't like the water, and I don't like to swim. I can't even help my kids with their homework, so how will I possibly be able to homeschool them? It became apparent shortly thereafter, however, that these barriers were all simply logistical. The logistics were hiding behind my fears, my pirates, as a huge change was staring me down—the opportunity to be able to travel and spend quality time with my family, notwithstanding it was in a way that was a complete about-face from the life I was currently living. We would have only limited Internet access and no cell phones. We'd be in really, really, really small quarters with just the four members of our immediate family. There'd be little contact with my extended family and friends. We had to survive making our own water and our own electricity. And the list went on.

One by one, I took a look at the fears. First, what do I do about not knowing how to sail? I took a sailing course, and I realized I knew more than I thought I knew. Having been racing and recreational sailing since he was a pre-teen, my husband is a very experienced sailor. I knew I'd be safe in his hands. To buffer my insecurity, we enlisted two very capable and experienced crew members for the first leg of our trip along the Pacific coast from San Diego to Cabo San Lucas, Mexico.

What about being uncomfortable on the water? It wasn't just seasickness, which I knew could dissipate after a few days of getting my sea legs. It was that I was a terra firma person. I loved adventure travel, but I preferred to do it by foot and on dry land. Whenever I'd stare out at the sea from the shore, it terrified me, as though it could swallow me up any time and I'd drown. The right boat was crucial for me to become comfortable and feel like I'd be okay. *Whatcha Gonna Do* was the perfect vessel. She is a stable catamaran, which doesn't heel over like a monohull does, and which would be important for the long passages. Also different than a monohull, the living space is above the water line, important for combatting sea sickness. She was sturdy and strong, and she did, indeed, take care of us. In return, we took care of her like no other home I've ever had. And in the process, I gained a respect for the ocean that was far more rooted in calm and trust than in terror. I've come to understand the ocean in a way I never had before. This personal growth for me was massive.

I also had to examine what it was about swimming that made me feel uncomfortable. I knew it wasn't a dissonance because the thought of becoming a proficient swimmer has always been a dream of mine. I realized that what I didn't like was being cold. Swimming in tropical waters is anything but cold. In fact, it is often the only way to get respite from the tropical heat. In addition, through our research, we discovered we would get to experience with our own eyes the most incredible coral reefs and wildlife. Indeed, we did, not to mention swimming with humpback whales and giant manta rays, sharks, and other wildlife of all shapes, sizes, and colors.

As for my kids, I researched what was involved in homeschooling. Clearly, other families cruised, so what did they do? In moving forward toward examining my fears, I came across an entire subculture of boaters, and boating families, who became encouraging resources throughout our two-and-a-half years cruising with kids. I was introduced to a homeschooling program that, while not optimal, was not Internet dependent and taught the basics of reading, writing, and arithmetic. We traded resources with other cruising families, homeschooled together, used other cruisers' expertise to teach us about music or birds or radios. Our kids learned firsthand about navigation, weather, sea life, electricity, making drinkable water, fishing, cooking without electrical appliances (which use too much power), cleaning toilets, doing laundry by hand, conversing with adults, socializing with kids older and younger than they were, and the list goes on. They were given responsibilities that most children their ages don't get because of the real-life safety issues at stake, like standing on the bow of our boat to direct us through coral reefs, driving the dinghy to run errands, taking radio control duties, and taking watch shifts. Although homeschooling was for me the most challenging part of our two-and-a-half years at sea, we managed. My kids successfully reintegrated into the school system when we re-entered life on land, and they got so much more learning and growth than had they stayed in their regular routines.

If you think you don't have the time, think again. You just haven't made it a priority. Because the truth of the matter is: You don't have the time to choose not to do it. You are getting closer to the end of your lifetime with every moment, and if you are not spending it moving toward what you were meant to be doing, to what keeps you feeling alive and fulfilled, to living your dreams, then you are simply wasting your time doing a whole lot of other things. You've made those other things a greater priority than being aligned with who you are.

As for money and resources, they may not be readily available, but there are certainly ways of finding them. If you are thinking that you are the exception, that resources are never available to you, then understand that those words are your pirates' words, not allowing you to find creative ways to find the resources you need.

There is no question that a dream has nothing realistic about it. Dreams are in the clouds, pie-in-the-sky, the ultimate. So how do you get from where you are now to where you want to be with your dreams? That's where the reality comes in. You must plan. And you must not let your pirates take over your ship.

Years ago, I met a woman who was a very dissatisfied attorney. In her quest for her big dream, she figured out that what she really wanted to do was to be a romance fiction novelist.

Her big pirate was disguising itself as a lack of money and time. She worked an 80 to 100 hour work week, so there most certainly was no extra time to write. She was making a great salary as an attorney, so how was she going to support her family if she quit her job and started writing novels, which weren't even guaranteed to sell? Her true pirates were saying, "This is just the way it is. You've made your bed. You started down this journey as an attorney, and you've accustomed your family to this way of living. You cannot turn your backs on them. Besides, you have no time in your busy career to write a novel. You only get a few weeks of vacation each year and cannot write a novel in that time, even if you were to sacrifice family vacation time, which, of course, you can't. You don't have the time or the financial wherewithal to go after what you really want."

Somehow, though, she was able to sit back and create this vision for herself as a successful novelist, and she got to the "Whatever It Takes" point. That's where her planning began: Working backwards, she decided that she needed a good salaried job with time off to write, and she came up with being a professor of literature. This had the added benefit of surrounding herself with English literature, which had always inspired her, as well as summers off that would allow her time to write her novels.

This plan to get her Ph.D. was going to take her about ten years if she went to school part-time while she continued to practice law. For many, this would seem daunting, and even insurmountable, but she realized ten years was going to pass whether or not she worked to achieve her dream. She was faced with a choice: Allow herself in ten years to be in the very same position she was in at that moment, doing what she disliked and depleted her, or she could take those ten years to start working toward what she really wanted to be doing, so when the invested time had passed, she'd be where she wanted to be. It would take hard work, but she knew the pay-off. She was not willing to go through life lamenting that she hadn't achieved her dream just because she wasn't willing to put in the time and effort.

There is not just one route to your dreams, either. What's important is to start moving toward it and see what comes up.

Remember my journey toward my own career change that I described in the last chapter? For years, I kept going back to the fact that I should have been a psychologist. I held onto that and mourned that it was just too late for me. I wasn't willing to go back to school for the years it was going to take. It was not until I finally succumbed to the dream that everything started to fall into place. In researching training programs, I found this relatively new field of coaching. Instantly, I knew. This was my dream. I haven't looked back since.

When our cruising friends mapped out their plan to spend quality time together as a couple while travelling, they did not know how to sail, they did not own a boat, and they had no money saved. Sounds a bit crazy to some, but they realized that sailing to the South Pacific could accomplish this dream very inexpensively. It took them only two years to save up enough money to buy a small sailboat and learn to sail proficiently. Then they took the leap. Sure, they lived frugally for two years, but they kept their vision at the forefront. Their plan was to find work in Australia or New Zealand, earn a bit more money so they could continue cruising, and keep on with the dream for as long as they could. When work became a bit more difficult to find overseas, they changed course, came home for a few months during the cyclone season, worked to earn more money to continue, and set out again.

Another family we came to know had decided that sailing for an extended period of time was their dream before kids even entered their lives. They researched what it would take logistically to go, and as a result, they came up with a seven-year plan once kids were born. They saved, they bought a boat, they got it ready, they knew when they had to put their house up for sale in order to leave when they wanted to, they worked on their writing careers, while still entrenched in their current jobs so they could earn income while cruising, and after seven years, they were off.

There are many other cruisers—singles, couples and families—who reach their dream of sailing the seas. For many, it takes upwards of ten years to realize the dream—to plan and figure out the logistics. Some sell their homes, scrimp and save, search near and far for the right boat, come to terms with what they'll do once they return to land, and so on. But one thing remains the same for all of them: The sailing is the dream, and although it seems crazy, the reality only comes into play in the planning. If you want it badly enough, the barriers to getting what you really want are simply logistical. And if you allow them to be the façade for your fear of going after what you really want, you will never get what you really want. Could you live with yourself knowing that the logistics got the better of you?

If you were on your deathbed tomorrow, would you be satisfied with all that you've accomplished?

If the answer is "no," then you must learn to slay your pirates in one of two ways: Confronting and then disarming them, or overcoming them by making them comparatively small.

Lessons three and four address these two methods of navigating your pirates. The first one has you getting to know your pirates so you can dispel their lies and send them to walk the plank. The second method has you create a vision of yourself and for yourself that is so compelling that it makes your pirates become small in comparison.

Here is what I know to be true: Had I not navigated around my own pirates and slain them, we would have missed out on the opportunity of a lifetime.

I don't know who named them swells. There's nothing swell about them. They should have named them awfuls.

-Hugo Vihlen (1931-)
Single-handed world record sailor

COFFEE TIME ON WGD

Who would have thought that coffee time aboard *Whatcha Gonna Do* would be so much fun?

At one time, Michael and I were trying to avoid coffee, trying to stay away from acquiring a physical addiction. Our friends aboard Britannia, Amanda and Krister, convinced us we've been looking at it all wrong. Coffee is a great pick-me-up in the morning, they said, and there's nothing wrong with having a cup or two in the a.m. Besides, coffee contains antioxidants.

And so we partake.

Two of my most memorable days of this trip involve coffee time with Piko and Britannia aboard WGD. The first was back in Taha'a in French Polynesia, when, on a rainy day (our biggest non-stop downpour to date), the Laurens and Krister/Amanda came over at 10 a.m. for what was supposed to be a cup of hot coffee. We added baguettes and French cheeses, and as time went on, we made a large pot of lentil soup. The party ended at 5 p.m. We watched back-to-back movies about global warming (*An Inconvenient Truth*, together with *The Great Global Warming Swindle*) and followed that with a heated *debate about whether, in fact, our oceans are melting and the world as we know it is coming to an end. We're still not sure.*

Two days ago, being the day we left Tonga, was the second such get-together. Piko and Britannia came over for a hot cuppa and crepes (with caramelized onions and cheese, or bananas and chocolate, no less!). This time the conversation centered around what we are all going to "do" once we get back to real life. It was quite personal, emotional, intense and amazing, all at the same time, as we focused on each one of us individually to talk about our dreams and our fears. The party ended at 3:30—only because we had to finish up the provisioning before heading out on our passage. This may, in fact, be our last get-together for quite some time, as Piko and Britannia are heading to New Zealand from Tonga in a few weeks, while we continue heading west for Australia. We've vowed to rendezvous again when we are all on the same continent for some more extended "chillaxing" together. The Pikos and the Britannias are like family.

Friendships are grown fast and intensely when you buddy boat, reminiscent of my childhood camp days. There's lots of love and laughter, sharing of ideas, dreams, boat parts, skills, and food, to name just a few. And, of course, coffee.

Coffee is a beautiful thing.

-Barb
En route Tonga to Fiji
17°53.33'S 177°45.96'W

LESSON 3:

Confronting Your Pirates:
Get Intimate With Them

The sea finds out everything you did wrong.

-Francis Stokes
American film director, screenwriter

Your pirates have been travelling with you practically from the beginning, and they will be part of you until the day you die. Until now, they have been so much a part of you that you think subconsciously whatever they say is truth. But is it really?

The only way to find out is to really listen to what your pirates have to say. This is completely counter to what we've been told: "You must not allow those negative thoughts into your head at all." The truth is, though, that as long as you are a living, breathing human being, you cannot avoid them. They are like the elephant in the room. Paying attention to them does not mean that you must accept them for the truth, but rather, in order to dispel their myths, you must actually know what you are fighting against.

Once you recognize what your pirates are saying, you can personify them, converse with them, and then send them away. This method can help "Confront and Disarm Your Pirates," so they no longer take over your ship.

December 6, 2010 | ## STARING INTO DARKNESS

It's 4:44 a.m., and I'm staring into darkness. I'm on watch for our 400-mile passage to Zihuatenajo. We are currently motor sailing as the True Wind speed is 2.7 knots coming from the North, which is directly behind us and too light to push us forward. With our starboard motor in overdrive (we only run one motor at a time), we are able to travel at over 8 knots (approx. 8 mph) running the engines at 2800 rpm. This is considered fast by sailboat standards. The engine temperature is around 180 degrees Celsius, which is good. Our autopilot is set at a course of 160 degrees, which is pretty much straight south. The radar screen stretching out to a 36-mile radius is completely blank, as it has been for the last several hours, with the exception of the Tres Marias islands off our starboard side (which our charts tell us to avoid as they are prison islands) and Isla Isabela, a bird sanctuary we visited when we were in the area last time, to our port. There is no moon, thus the darkness. Way up, the stars are incredibly vivid. Straight behind us, in the wake of the engine, bursts of phosphorescence illuminate the water. Other than that, it is difficult to see where the horizon is, where the ocean meets the sky. Given that we have a navigation station inside the cabin, I am able to monitor things in the warmth of the salon, but every 10 minutes or so, I go outside to do a quick check—temperature gauge on the engines are still looking good, sail is still looking good, and around us is still looking, well, dark. Not sure what I'm looking at in the vicinity. That's where your faith in your vessel and God come in. We hope it's not our turn to hit a lost container fallen from a container ship. We are very aware that most "bad" things happen at night, but that's where we give up our control. We make sure someone is on watch at all times, we make sure our boat is in good sea-going shape, we wait for "weather windows" before departing on a passage, we have our emergency procedures in place and our "ditch" bags at the ready (the bags that you take with you when you have to ditch the boat, i.e., it's sinking), and the rest is up to the powers that be.

As we lie in bed trying to regain our rest for our next watch, we listen to every creak and sound that the boat makes. I'm still not totally used to these noises. Some of them sound like the boat is going to crack apart. Occasionally, a wave comes and hits the inside of the hull and practically knocks me out of bed. Intellectually, I know that this vessel can take much more than that, and hopefully much more than what we'll ever experience if we are prudent, but still the sounds are amplified inside the hulls, where we lie awake listening. Anything out of the ordinary and we jump up to question whoever is on watch.

The engine is purring after our 1,000-hour service which had brought us to Mazatlan, where the only Yanmar-authorized mechanic in Mexico is located. Many boats have Yanmar motors, so you'd think there'd be more authorized mechanics around, but TIM (This Is Mexico)...

And like most things boat-related and/or Mexico-related, it took much longer than expected. I thought we were being conservative when we estimated we'd be in Mazatlan a week, and we left after two. Parts had to be shipped to Guadalajara for repair and service, new parts were ordered from elsewhere, and the engines were literally taken apart and put back together. This in and of itself is a cause for anxiety: The engines were working well before, but now that they've been tinkered with, what if they haven't been put back together properly? There was recently a sailboat that sank in the South Pacific, due to a massive leak around the drive shaft after it had just been serviced, due to faulty workmanship. Again, we try to be prudent, and the rest is up to the powers that be.

Time for me to pop outside to check the darkness, although the sky to our port is brightening up a bit by now, and I can start making out the eastern horizon. No sight of land, though, as we are more than 30 miles offshore. At least this far off, we hope to avoid fishing lines and running aground ...

-Barb, at 21 degrees 08.713 minutes North by 105 degrees 53.244 minutes West

As we were setting out to go cruising, we got cold feet more than once. Our fears were huge: We are destroying our kids. They will never recover socially, academically, emotionally after we take them away from their school friends, from their "normal" education, and from everything they know. And what about our safety? We were crazy to be putting our family into harm's way. We could DIE out there! We are being irresponsible and selfish just because we had this dream. And because I didn't even know how to sail, if Michael went overboard, I would not be able to save him. Or worse yet, if I couldn't save him, I would never be able to get the boat with my kids to safety. And, even if we were to survive, we'd be doomed once we got back to our old lives. We wouldn't get jobs. We would not be able to live and provide for our family. We'd be complete and utter failures.

Pirates? Without a doubt, yes. Had we taken them for our truth, we would never have set out on our adventure.

One way to dispel the myths that your pirates tell you is to educate yourself, get resourceful, and plan. Let's take what was our ultimate pirate: "You could DIE out there." We had to approach this pirate by fleshing out the fears. It stemmed from the fear that our boat would sink and we would drown.

Here's what we did know: The likelihood of a catamaran sinking is very slim. The hulls are built with individually sealed compartments, so if one is punctured, the others will keep the boat afloat. There is a possibility (although still slight), however, of the boat flipping upside down, and even then, if we had to wait in the water, we'd be safe by hanging onto the jack lines running underneath the boat, and we had a life raft. If the life raft were to fail, we'd have a second chance with our dinghy to climb into. If there was a fire, we had fire extinguishers and fire blankets. If we would have to abandon ship in that or any other scenario, once again, we were prepared with a life raft *and* a dinghy. We had an abandon-ship plan, where each of us was assigned a specific item to take when leaving the boat: Two rescue beacons, a satellite phone, and an abandon ship bag, to name just a few.

Wednesday, November 2, 2011 | # DITCH BAG MANIFESTO

Any well-prepared cruising boat should have an abandon-ship bag at the ready, just in case its crew needs to, you guessed it, abandon ship for any reason. We know that leaving our boat is very unlikely. First, it means that our catamaran, which is built so that it doesn't sink, would have to sink. Second, even if it does flip upside down, leaving one's boat for the life raft should always be a last ditch decision, as it's much easier to be spotted by a rescue boat or aircraft if you are with your boat due to its relative size.

Notwithstanding all of that, IF we were to ditch our boat and head into the life raft, we are prepared to be out there, as uncomfortable as it may be.

In preparing our ditch bags, we realized that with four people, we had to split its contents into two bags. One of them is the "priority" bag with the more important items. And because the bags don't float, we've wrapped them in life jackets, and enclosed all its contents into waterproof ziplocked bags. The bags are kept at our navigation station inside the cabin whenever we are underway, so that they can be easily grabbed on our way out the door, so to speak.

In addition to these bags, we have reviewed other items that we need to take: Two EPIRBs (Emergency Personal Identification Rescue Beacons, which send off a signal to the coast guard), our sheath knife and leatherman tool, water bottles, spear gun, and, of course, life jackets (which should be worn at that stage).

After much research, here are the contents of our ditch bags:

Flares
Green dye marker
Satellite phone (recharged the 1st of every month)
VHF radios (fully charged at the start of every passage)
GPS
Extra batteries for all electronics
Waterproof flashlight
Head lamp
Binoculars
Various Tupperware containers
Various Ziploc bags, plastic bags
Rain ponchos x4
Umbrella
Baseball hats x4
Wool hats x2
Sunglasses
Toilet paper

Sanitary napkins, tampons
Plastic wrap (1 roll)
Tin foil
Sponges x2
Pocket Knife
Rope
Strong tape (duct tape)
Waterproof matches
Wooden stick
Safety pins
Clothespins
Emergency blankets (foil) x4
Notepads and pens/pencils
Game book
Deck of cards
"Adrift" (book about being lost at sea for 76 days)
Passport copies
$100 Cash
Immunization records

Credit Card
Diver DAN emergency
numbers
Fishing equipment:
50 lb monofilament line
2 weights, 2 lures, 1
floaty
10 lb test line
Leaders
Food:
12 power bars
4 cans sardines
Gatorade
1 gallon water
First aid:
Sunscreen 45 SPF
Staff infection antibiotic
Triangle slingband
SAM splint

Dry skin lotion
Tensor bandage
Bandage tape
Bandaids
Burn cream
Alcohol swabs
Polysporin
Blistex lip treatment
Zinc oxide
Antiseptic wash
Artificial tears eye drops
Non-stick first aid pads
Sting meds: lanacaine,
claritin
Pain meds: vicodin,
tylenol with codeine
Seasickness meds:
dramamine, meclizine,
scopalomine

Have we missed anything? Other items recommended by the author of Adrift, who was stuck in his life raft for 76 days before being found thousands of miles later: rudder, closed cell foam cushion, and sail fabric.

It would be difficult to carry enough fresh water onto a life raft as it is heavy and cumbersome. We have practiced creating a solar still to make fresh water from salt water using the Tupperware container, plastic wrap, and a weight ...

Some might find it curious that we've included things like pad and pencils, a deck of cards, and a game book. Apparently, the biggest issue for surviving life in a life raft after getting fresh water is one's mental state. We'll take care of that one by having a games tournament ...

We certainly don't intend to spend very long in a life raft, especially given all the chances we've given ourselves to make sure that help is on the way as soon as possible (two EPIRBs and a satellite phone). Nonetheless, it sure gives us a lot more comfort knowing that we are prepared.

-Barb, comfortably on board Whatcha Gonna Do
Day 3 passage Vanuatu to Chesterfield Reef,
New Caledonia
18 degrees 59.217 minutes South
162 degrees 00.297 minutes East

If we were to need to abandon ship, would we be uncomfortable for possibly a few days? Yes. But would we die? Likely not. In fact, we would be more likely to die in a car crash getting to our boat than we would be to die at sea.

In order to overcome our fears of not being able to support ourselves when we got back, we began with the education, resourcefulness, and planning method. We made sure that we had enough savings to keep us going for a couple of years upon our return, and we trusted that we'd be able to sell our boat at the end of the cruising experience.

In addition, we used a second method to overcome our fear of being destitute upon our return, that of getting intimate with our pirates by going all the way down our path of fears with them. It looked like this:

What if we don't get jobs? Answer: we have our savings for two years.

What if we don't get jobs for two years? Then what? Answer: Two years is a long time to be without a job where we live, so it's not likely; but even if it were, we'd have to move.

What if we have to move? Then what? Answer: We've moved before, and we managed.

What if we get so poor that we'll have to live on the streets? Then what? This became the point at which I felt like I was arguing in circles, getting sucked into the vortex of going nowhere, but just spiraling for the sake of standing my ground.

It wasn't just the spiraling negativity that had me walk away from my pirates. This was the point at which my pirates' incredulity appeared—perhaps way down the path, but still, ultimately, the ridiculousness of the fear became apparent. We do not believe we will ever get to a place of being homeless and living on the street. Period. Is there even the slightest possibility that we would end up on the streets, homeless, jobless, and destitute? Yes, but the chances are so unlikely that in weighing out the risk, we realized we would be crazy not to seize the opportunity to take a sailing sabbatical.

The idea is to go down the path of your fears until you find the ultimate fear that lies underneath it all. In the safety scenario, our ultimate pirate was telling us we could die; in the poverty scenario, our underlying pirate told us we'd end up on the street. In both scenarios, the chances were so slim that we were able to dispel the myths our pirates were telling us.

In situations where there might be the slightest amount of truth to what our pirates are saying, like the possibility of dying out at sea or ending up jobless and homeless and living on the streets, we must balance it out against the compelling nature of living our dreams according to our passions. Once you can come to terms with the nonsensical side of your pirates, you have disarmed them and then can send them away.

When we get into a car, there is a slight chance that we will get into a car accident and die. We take precautions, which is the knowledge and planning part: We don't speed, we slow down in bad weather, and we wear seatbelts. Going down the path of fears takes us to actually dying as result of the car accident. The risk is heavily outweighed by the need to get from point A to point B. The latter is more compelling to us than the fear of dying in a car crash.

By getting to know what our pirates have been telling us, we are able to send those pirates walking the plank. Exercises at the end of this chapter can help you get to know your pirates, so you can recognize what they have been saying to you all this time, dispel their myths, and send them far, far away.

Here's what I know to be true: When your pirates show up (and they will), and they tell you their usual story, you must be ready with your response.

He that will not sail till all dangers are over
must never put to sea.

-Thomas Fuller (1608-1661)
English writer and historian

EXERCISE:
Getting Acquainted With Your Pirates

---

1. Who are Your Pirates?

Write a biography of one of your pirates, and regardless of what that (or any other) pirate is saying to you, the idea is to have fun with it. You will see that there is a little bit of humor in the fact that you've actually been taking him or her seriously.

- Name of your pirate:

- This is how your pirate looks, sounds, and comes across (physical description, gender, appearance, voice, size, dress, airs):

- This is what your pirate likes to do whenever you are around:

- Your pirate's behavior when you are not paying attention to him or her includes:

- When you are around for your pirate, his or her favorite sayings or stories he or she has for you are:

- Your pirate's strongest skills and abilities include:

- Your pirate is at the top of his or her game when he or she feels like this:

- Your pirate steps on these important values and aspirations:

- Your pirate's own secret fear is:

- Your pirate believes it is an essential part of your life because:

2. Converse and Respond

List your pirates—as many as you can—in the left-hand column of the chart on the next page.

Next, pretend that your closest, dearest friend has come to you with these pirates as his or her own. In the right-hand column, write the responses you'd give to your friend. Speak to the truth about your friend's (your) abilities, magnificence, and strengths. Include the reasons why your friend's (your) pirates should not stop him or her from achieving their goals.

In this way, you are conversing with your pirates and really listening to what they have to say. By responding to yourself as you would to a friend who shares your very same pirates, you can really get to the bottom of why you shouldn't be listening to them any longer.

PIRATES:	MY RESPONSES:

3. Get Clear on What Your Pirates are Costing You

List your pirates—as many as you can—in the left-hand column of the chart on the next page.

Next, for each pirate, identify:

1. What's true about what your pirates are telling you? How are your pirates protecting you?

2. If you listen to your pirates and maintain your status quo, what is it costing you? What are you missing out on?

3. What do you want to say to that pirate to disarm it and send it away? What will you say to bring yourself to your highest state of being, your biggest, truest self?

Pirate	How It Protects Me / What's True Here?	What is It Costing Me?	This is How I Can Disarm It / My Response

4. Your Personal Truth

From getting personal with your pirates, what do you know? Will you continue to allow your pirates to run your life? Journal here about what you know and what you want for yourself.

THE BREATH OF PASSAGE MAKING

So many sailors cringe at the thought of overnight passages. Anxiety takes over them days before in anticipation of boredom, monotony, loss of freedom, imprisonment. Not me. I look forward to passages—and the longer the better. Sure, lack of sleep (we take turns being on watch 24/7) is a form of torture, but after a few days, one gets used to the routine.

And it's the routine that I embrace. Call me crazy. Back on land, living the "normal" life, I would often plan for stepping out of routine, knowing that without the effort I'll be way too complacent in my life. Cruising on a boat, however, has me living out of my comfort zone, on the edge, so much so that it overshadows any routine we create. In fact, cruising feels much more like a life of constant challenge than I ever imagined.

Several years ago, I completed an exercise listing my top "values" (states of being that I must have in my life in order to feel at the top of my game, fulfilled, living my best self) and one of those was, "Order/routine with spurts of adventure and newness." Hmmmm. Without the passages, my life looks a lot more like "adventure and newness with spurts of order/routine." With a full house (or shall I say boat), I have little time while cruising to sit back and just breathe. Breathing is necessary to regroup, take stock, recharge. Without it, I'm just plain hyperventilating.

I often liken passage making to being stuck at home during a snow storm. It places your life on pause. All appointments are canceled. You eat what you've got in the house. You hang out with your family. You can clean out your closet. You can nap during the day. The whole world slows down. It's peaceful. It gives you time to think. What's next? What's been working and what hasn't?

Plus passage making allows me to do what I do well: organize. Sounds rather order-like, no? Are you getting it?... You see, there's a lot out here that I don't do well: sailing still hasn't become second nature to me (although I'm getting better!), homeschooling is less than stellar (we have only a couple more months to go!), housekeeping is, well, a chore, and I don't have my work that I love and keeps me fulfilled. But passages, if they are to go smoothly, require lists. And lists I'm good at. I create lists of watch schedules, lists of what the kids need to accomplish in homeschooling before we make the next landfall, and lists of what food we need to get rid of before quarantine at the next country takes it all away. And my meal plans are so beautiful—meaning we eat well and we eat healthy—and I spend a lot of my time checking produce to avoid spoilage, pulling out food that requires prep for the following day's meals, or baking bread to greet the kids when they awaken. Who knew that this would be what keeps me grounded while living on a boat? On land, the monotony of it would make me cringe.

And then I step outside at 2 a.m. on my watch to check that all is running smoothly, and right in front of me as the wind hits my face and I smell the sea air, I see a sliver of an orange moon rising into a clear starry-filled night. And I take a deep, recharging, peaceful breath.

-Barb, en route Tanna Island to Port Vila, Vanuatu

LESSON 4:

Overcoming Your Pirates:
Create a Compelling Destination

There is nothing like lying flat on your back on the deck, alone except for the helmsman aft at the wheel, silence except for the lapping of the sea against the side of the ship. At that time, you can be equal to Ulysses and brother to him.

-Errol Flynn (1909-1959)

Your pirates are no match for your biggest and truest self, for your life purpose, your mission, or your compelling dream. You can blow right past your pirates, then, if you can live as close to your highest biggest self as possible, or create a compelling vision and develop a mission that is far bigger than your pirates. In fact, nearly half of the respondents to my survey on making successful change indicated that creating a compelling goal helped them achieve a prior success.

The result of using this strategy is to dwarf your pirates to the point of not even mattering and thus being easy to ignore. You realize you are not serving anyone by being small. Your vision becomes so clear and so essential to you that it is like the air you breathe, so that, because it is so compelling, you cannot imagine yourself not doing it. Your vision becomes your personal mission, defining who you are and something that you *must* do.

Thursday, November 10, 2011 | # FINAL APPROACH

We are now less than 50 miles from making landfall in Australia. The seas are calm—as in flat calm—and there is less than 10 knots of wind with a full moon. We have the massive kite-like spinnaker sail pulling us forward peacefully at a slow 3.5 knots (roughly equivalent to 3.5 miles per hour). We see the lighthouse's signal in the distance, almost whispering, "You've just about made it." We've covered thousands of miles, visited numerous countries and cultures, met countless people, and survived small quarters with our family of four.

It's hard to believe. The retrospective begins.

- Barb
40 miles from Bundaberg, Queensland, Australia
24 degrees 19.170 minutes South
152 degrees 55.491 minutes East

You must get past your pirates so you can live your dreams, aspirations, and mission. The vision of yourself as your biggest highest self or of your own personal mission is like the mountain beyond the boulder in the river scenario; it is so huge, so compelling, that you don't even notice the boulder that's right in front of you.

Isn't a vision only for spiritual people? What if I'm not very spiritual?

Whether you want to call your compelling destination a vision, a mission, or a dream, it's necessary to have an end result in mind in order to know where you are going. With a vision in mind, your decisions are more intentional as you can know whether what you are doing is in service of your end goal. Any successful person, spiritual or not, must know where they are going before they set out.

That's not to say that the route cannot change. On the contrary, you must remain flexible to variations and deviations on your way. But when you set out, you need to set a course and get started. While you are en route, you get to assess and evaluate where you are headed. In fact, the assessment and evaluation are key to getting to where you want to go.

Spiritual or not, a destination is essential.

How do I overcome my pirates so that I can, in fact, ignore them?

We cannot be successful in ignoring our deep-rooted fears that manifest themselves as pirates without a strategy. Your pirates will continue to resurface, but unless you can create something that is far bigger than they are, it will be difficult to overcome them.

If you get yourself grounded into your biggest, most magnificent self, and then create a vision for yourself that is so compelling, you will become a giant next to your pirates. Your pirates will seem so small that they will be insignificant in comparison.

To begin, in order to become your biggest, most magnificent self, you must honor your values. Values are those feeling states that you must have in your life in order to feel fulfilled, such as accomplishment, collaboration, or expertise, to name only a very few. Your values are not good or bad; there's no judgment to them. They are not what you think you *should* be like, but rather what, in fact, has you feel fully alive. The best starting point for setting yourself up for success and being able to ignore your pirates is to identify your values and begin honoring them by "doing" things that will ensure you bring those "being" states into your life.

Note that when you feel fulfilled and alive, it does not necessarily mean you are happy. For example, when I was sitting beside my father in the hospital after he suffered a heart attack, I was far from happy about his state of health, but I felt fulfilled being there, like it was the exact place that I needed and wanted to be at that moment, doing what I felt was aligned with who I was.

THINGS THAT MAKE ME HAPPY

Sunday, December 11, 2011

What makes me happy has been on my mind lately as I read Gretchen Rubin's The Happiness Project, about a year in the author's life in which she consciously takes on things that she hopes will make her happier. She spends January focusing on getting to sleep earlier, exercising more, and cleaning out her closets, all in the hopes that they will boost her energy (they do). In February, she focuses on doing things to improve her relationship with her husband, including trying not to expect so much acknowledgment (it doesn't work). And so on. The book demonstrates an interesting way of approaching what I call not the search for happiness, but rather fulfillment, that state of being in which you are feeling at the top of your game.

The topic has also had me thinking loads lately as we prepare to re-enter regular life after almost two and a half years of living on the fringe. It's important that we map it out carefully to make it as smooth as possible for us all. A few weeks back, my friend, Diane, posed the question to several of us: What do we want to take back to regular life that we've gained while on this journey? For many who take on an adventure like ours, the trip is a conscious effort to get away from a life in which work reigns, family time is rare, and stress is too great, and so it's clear what they are wanting to last into their life on land after their respective journeys are over. It made me realize that I really loved my life before we left. Sure, I had my own share of issues day-to-day, but I've worked really hard at creating a life in which I took care of my needs and I worked to my strengths. I would consciously work on anything that wasn't "working for me" and improve it with single step actions.

If the truth be told, and while I loved this trip and wouldn't have missed it for the world, the last nine months have been challenging. The problem was that I had focused so much on being in the moment and catering to everyone else's needs that I forgot about my own. Don't get me wrong. It's been incredible. But I have, in the midst of it, forgotten about so many of the things that I must have in my life in order to feel fulfilled and happy.

And so when we spent three of the last five days hiking in the Blue Mountains of New South Wales, it was exhilarating to realize that hiking makes me so happy. I'll have to be sure to remember this as we settle back into life on land.

Other areas that will need to be worked to get back to that place of fulfillment: Alone time with Michael. Looking after myself with exercise and taking alone time. Getting my career back on track. Do Yoga. Stop complaining. Go to sleep earlier. Avoid clutter.

Once home, even little steps toward these goals will surely make me happy. And I'm already happy about the plan.

-Barb
Brisbane, Queensland, Australia

When you're feeling inspired and at the top of your game, you're far more likely to make important changes. You feel so much bolder to make the changes than if you weren't feeling satisfied and you weren't feeling fulfilled. By incorporating values into your day-to-day life by rituals, or "doing" your values, you are already on your path toward your dreams, in addition to jumpstarting your confidence in believing you can achieve what you set your mind to, even as your pirates show up.

Exercises are provided at the end of this chapter to help you discover your own values so that you live in alignment, with fulfillment, which will ultimately help propel you toward living your dream and setting yourself up for success. They will, in turn, help you get in touch with your biggest, most magnificent self.

In addition, exercises have been included at the end of this chapter to have you consider yourself in the future. When we can imagine ourselves in the future, we see ourselves as wiser, calmer, more trusting versions of our current selves. When we listen to ourselves in the future, our voices are much stronger than our pirates' voices. In fact, our pirates may even be completely absent.

Another exercise will have you recount how you uniquely show up in the world. When you really think about what you are good at, what others appreciate about you, or what has you feeling alive at the top of your game, you become much, much bigger than you are when your pirates are shooting you down. It will take some work, but if you can create a personal mantra that reminds you of who you really are, of your uniqueness and your gifts, to be repeated whenever you begin to hear your pirates as you approach an important change, you can change your mindset and overcome your pirates.

Perhaps the most compelling method of overcoming your pirates, however, is to create a vision for yourself in line with your life purpose or mission—what it is that you dream for yourself. This strategy allows you to ignore your pirates by blowing right past them with a vision that is much bigger than all your pirates together. Your pirates are no match for you being your true self, living your life's purpose, and achieving your ultimate goals and mission.

What is a Vision for Success?

We all want to know that our most precious resource, our time on this planet, is not wasted. We want to know that each moment counts and we are in choice in how we spend that time. Yet, often we set out to accomplish tasks without being conscious of their purpose.

In order to measure whether we make each moment count, we must understand *what* our tasks are *in service of.* We'll call this purpose our **vision**, or our mission. A Vision for Success then uses **milestones** as assessment tools for measuring how you're doing on your journey toward your vision. **Goals** are then created as the necessary steps to move you forward, putting one foot in front of the other, until you achieve what you are aspiring to.

It looks something like this:

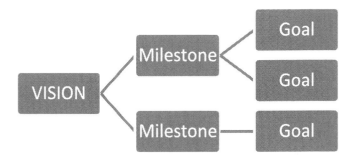

1. Vision

Beginning first with your **vision**, it is how you see your life if you were living as your future self, as your biggest, highest, and best self, as if you have achieved everything you have ever dreamed of. Interestingly, it is a vision not of material things, necessarily, but of a state of being. It can be considered your "destination," what you have created for yourself, your family, your community, the world around you, and, in turn, how each of them sees and relates to you.

For example: *I am wildly successful at my career and am seen as the expert, evidenced by the numerous individuals I have impacted. I clearly set the boundaries around my work in a resonant way, so I am fully present with my family and look after myself so I am healthy and comfortable. I am grateful for the bounty of life.*

Note that there is no statement in this vision resembling a dollar figure for my income. This leaves it open as to how "wildly successful" is defined. The material or tangible things will be considered my milestones or goals, so they can be adjusted along the way.

WHY WE ARE DOING THIS

I've come across a book, entitled "Adrift: Seventy-six Days Lost At Sea," by Steven Callahan. ...In the opening pages, he has aptly stated (and in better words than I ever could) why we took off on this adventure.

"I wish I could describe the feeling of being at sea, the anguish, frustration, and fear, the beauty that accompanies threatening spectacles, the spiritual communion with creatures in whose domain I sail. There is a magnificent intensity in life that comes when we are not in control but are only reacting, living, surviving ... [F]or me, to go to sea is to get a glimpse of the face of God. At sea I am reminded of my insignificance - of all men's insignificance. It is a wonderful feeling to be so humbled."

I have found this quote particularly compelling. Interestingly, my own vision begins as follows:

"I am inspired and alive, completely aware of the wonders and awe of everything around me. I am deeply connected to the past, as well as to the future, fully aware of my place in this universe (both great and small; both physically and in time). My inner voice is strong and clear and guides me to live life fully. I move through life with a sense of purpose. I receive abundant blessings."

And boy, do I ever. So far, so good.

-Barbara
Signing off from Nuevo Vallarta, Nayarit, Mexico

---

2. Milestones

After creating a Vision for Success, we need to check in along the way to make sure we are on the right path toward that vision. As noted above, these check-ins are our **milestones**, which will be the result of a culmination of goals having been met and the interim markers along the path toward our vision that help us determine whether we are achieving what we have planned. Milestones can be used to measure our progress and evaluate the effectiveness of our actions and goals.

What makes a milestone unique is that it describes a moment or snapshot in time, a clear picture, that indicates you have achieved a certain moment on your path to your vision. It begins by stating the date in the future at which you wish to create a milestone—at one year or other regular intervals—and sets out the snapshot in time, and by its nature, describes what you are doing, how you are feeling, and what you are learning or realizing. For example: "It is now April 1, 2011, and I am checking my provisioning inventory." This picture shows me that I am planning for a Pacific crossing, that I am excited but scared (and slightly overwhelmed), but that I'm really doing it. Your milestones need only make sense to you, being a picture that you understand and has a particular significance for you.

3. Goals

Finally, we use the term **goal** as the single, actionable, and measurable steps that *you* set for yourself in order to move forward to reach your milestones.

Before setting your goals, be prepared that if you do not achieve one or more of them, then it may be because of one of two reasons. The first may be that you are not fully resonant with it and, therefore, not feeling that "Whatever It Takes" instinct. If this is the case, it's okay to realign yourself. The second reason may be because the action was not appropriate to achieve your goal. Step back, evaluate, and revamp your plan when necessary.

Effective goal setting begins with the SMART acronym to develop the actionable steps necessary to achieve your milestones and, ultimately, your vision or mission:

Specific: Goals should be as specific as possible. When you say your goal, a clear picture of what it looks like should emerge. If you create a goal that contains more than one step, break it down into its smallest actionable steps. Each step must be specific enough to create a measurable result; either you have achieved it, or you have not.

E.g., if the project is creating an Emergency Sail Plan, break it down: Choose a close and reliable contact on land; choose a reliable backup contact on land; speak to those contacts to describe routing plans and timing; decide the amount of time that should pass before contacts call the Coast Guard; provide registration details of EPIRBs to the US Coast Guard.

Measurable: Goals must be measurable so progress can be evaluated objectively. Any person must be able to clearly say whether or not you've achieved it.

E.g., provisioning enough food for the crossing cannot be assessed objectively and, therefore, is not measurable, since "enough" to one sailor is different from another. It would, therefore, be a judgment call whether you've achieved it or not. Purchasing 15 jars of pasta sauce would be measurable. You've either done it, or you haven't.

Achievable/Attainable: Your goal must feel achievable if you are to be motivated to take the necessary action steps. Do you have the tools, resources, and skills necessary to achieve the goal? If not, how will you go about obtaining these? Can you start and maintain the achievement of this goal yourself?

E.g., getting a particular person to be part of your crew is not completely in your control, because that person may not be willing or able to join your crew. A goal of getting a crew member who has sailed the route before is more achievable (although, of course, you can include your preference in your goal).

Resonant: Your goal must be something you can commit to in your gut, something compelling enough for you that you really want to achieve it, even if it is stretching you. Keep it in the positive.

Note that even if the actionable step seems tedious to you, you can achieve it if it helps you to reach a vision that is resonant for you.

Time-framed: Your goals should come with some reasonable expectation on when they will be achieved. Be sure to attach a deadline to it.

Here's what I know to be true: Getting big so you are living as your biggest, most magnificent self, together with creating a vision, are powerful tools toward getting what you really want in life. Combined with milestones established for assessing where you are and goals to keep you in action and moving forward, you can blow past your pirates and make your leap.

Ships are the nearest thing to dreams
that hands have ever made.

-Robert N. Rose
Poet

EXERCISE:
Discovering Your Values

The next page contains a sample list of values or feeling states that you may identify as necessary to have in your life in order to feel fulfilled and fully alive. This list can be used as an aid for the exercises that follow to help you discover your own values.

Sample Values List

Accomplishment	Empowerment	Motivation
Acknowledgment	Freedom	Nature
Adventure	Faith	Order
Appreciation	Family	Obligation
Affiliation	Fun	Oneness
Artistic Expression	Friendship	Pleasure
Admiration	Generosity	Predictability
Authority	Gratitude	Prestige
Autonomy	Goodness	Positive
Aliveness	Harmony	Power
Authenticity	Health	Quiet
Balance	Helping	Realistic
Beauty	Humor	Renewal
Challenge	High Earnings	Recognition
Community	Honesty	Respect
Compassion	Humanitarian	Responsibility
Competence	Humility	Risk-taking
Competition	Hopeful	Self-Discipline
Calm	Independence	Self-Restraint
Contribution	Impactful	Service
Control	Inclusiveness	Spirituality
Courage	Inspiration	Simplicity
Cooperation	Influence	Stability
Creativity	Integrity	Status
Communication	Joy	Synthesis
Connection	Justice	Structure
Curiosity	Knowledge	Team Work
Collaboration	Knowing	Tenacity
Diversity	Leadership	Tranquility
Duty	Learning	Trust
Energy	Love	Truth
Enthusiasm	Loyalty	Transparency
Excellence	Liberation	Variety
Entrepreneurial	Meaning	Wisdom
	Moderation	Wonder

Exercise: Discovering Your Values (cont'd)

1. Think about a time in your life where you felt like you were at the top of your game, experiencing something particularly poignant for you—a snapshot that has stuck in your mind over time. What were you doing? How were you feeling? What made it especially rewarding or fulfilling for you? Who were you being?

   For example, during our three-week Pacific crossing, I took the 1 a.m. to 6 a.m. watch. This was by choice, as it allowed me quiet time to blog, adjust sails, and tidy the salon. The snapshot I keep in my mind is the sun rising up behind the boat, with nothing but water surrounding us, hearing the lapping of waves, seeing the sails full, feeling the wind in my face, having the salon tidy, and an introspective blog post complete. From this you can glean some of my top values: beauty, peacefulness, calm, accomplishment, meaning, unexpected connection, organization, and independence.

   Describe your snapshot here:

   Now list the values that can be identified from your description here:

2. What's the most meaningful thing you did this week? Why was it important? And why was that important? Keep asking why that was important with each answer until you cannot take it further.

   For example, the most meaningful thing I did last week was hike with a friend. That was important because we hadn't connected in a long time. That was important because she's a good friend and I want to nurture the relationship. That was important because I love her and love supporting her to feel good about herself. That was important because it makes me feel like I make a difference to her. That is important because I need to feel like I have impact. Why is that important? Because she acknowledges me and makes me feel good about myself. From this example, you can hear the following values: connection, generosity, supporting, love, appreciation, contribution, impact, acknowledgment.

   Write your story here:

   Now list the values that can be identified from your story here:

3. Name three people you admire. Why did you choose these people? What do you think are the values they honor, especially the ones that you admire?

Person #1:
Their Values:

Person #2:
Their Values:

Person #3:
Their Values:

4. What do you love to do? Why? What are the feeling states that you get from doing them? List some of them here:

Love to Do	Why/Values It Honors

5. What do you hate to do? What gets you really mad? What are the values/feeling states that are missing or are in conflict with these things? What values are being stepped on by these things?

Hate to Do	Why/Value That's Missing

Gets Me Mad	Why/Value That's Compromised

6. What fulfils you? What are your passions?

EXERCISE:
Honoring Your Values

From all the values you listed in the exercises above, choose your top 10 to 15 and list them on the left side of the chart on the following page. This column represents a way of *being* that brings you a feeling of fulfillment.

On the right-hand side of the chart, opposite each value, list the things you can *do* to bring about that feeling state on a day-to-day basis.

Value	What I Can Do to Honor This Value
E.g. Connection	2 of 4 Saturday date nights/month with my husband; 2 lunches/month with my friends; Private time with each child at pick up or bedtime at least 5 times/week

EXERCISE:

Getting Big

Your responses to these prompts should be referenced often as you approach a change, especially when you begin to hear your pirates telling you that you should maintain your status quo.

1. Use Your Values to Get Big

When you are grounded in your values, you are more powerful and resolved.

Review your top values. Then respond to these prompts:

- These are the values I most want to recall when my pirates show up:

- What must I do to maintain those states of being as I move forward toward taking a leap and living my dreams?

2. Get Acquainted with Yourself in the Future to Get Big Today

If your cell phone was to ring and it was you, 20 years from now, what would your future self say to you about going after what you really want? What does your future self tell you about who you really are?

What does your future self tell you about what to focus on over the next 20 years?

3. Get in Touch with Your Biggest, Most Magnificent Self

When you are using your unique gifts, you are doing what you were put on this earth to do. You are serving your purpose by using your gifts.

Answer these questions to identify with your biggest self in the context of going after what you really want:

- What's really important to me is:

- What I really want is:

- Who I really am is:

- What I was born to do is:

- What I do really well is:

- My unique gift(s) is/are:

Now consider this:

When I am at the top of my game, I am _____. It is not serving me to play small.

I get to choose what I really want, what brings me joy, fulfillment, and aliveness. What I really want is:

_____.

What brings me joy, fulfillment, and aliveness is:

_____.

4. Create Your Own Personal Mantra

Based upon answers to the prompts above, develop some phrases or sentences that will serve as your own personal mantra to repeat to yourself as you begin to hear your pirates' voices emerge.

EXERCISE:

Creating Your Vision for Success

Step 1: Writing Your Vision:

Tips for writing a vision:

- Write in present tense, as if you have already reached the vision. If you write about something in the future, you will keep it in the future; if you write about wanting something, you will manifest more wanting.

- Go after what you really want, not what you think you can get.

- "How" you get there doesn't matter and comes after the "what." The "how" becomes apparent with each step you take and is not a question of resources, but one of resourcefulness. The "how" is in the logistics.

- Focus on non-tangibles, which leaves greater flexibility in how things transpire.

- Let it flow from your heart and don't get too analytical. Don't worry about grammar or wording; you can go back and polish it later.

- Your vision is the unique expression of who you are. Some visions are simple, some poetic, some more visual, some longer. Some even include a symbol or drawing if it feels important.

Begin first by grounding yourself. Do this by writing about the qualities and values that are important to you by thinking about:

- WHO is your future self, and how does she or he show up in your vision? What is the atmosphere around him or her? What is he or she like? How does he or she relate to others? To his or her community and his or her world? Use your future self as a guiding light of what is important to you.

- How does your vision FEEL? Describe the energy, how people are relating to each other and to you, and the feeling states that bring you this energy.

- WHAT have you produced in your vision? Describe the results for you, for your family, for the world at large, and your legacy.

- WHY have you done all this? What is the higher purpose of your work, the expression of who you want to be at your highest, most powerful self?

Write your vision here, and be sure to refer back to it often to keep you on your way and your pirates at bay:

Step 2: Setting Your Milestones

As with your vision, milestones are stated in present tense form.

These are the milestones you are committing to:

Five years in the future:
It is (date) _____, and I am (describe the snapshot)

_____

_____

_____

Three years in the future:
It is (date) _____, and I am (describe the snapshot)

_____

_____

_____

One year in the future:
It is (date) _____, and I am (describe the snapshot)

_____

_____

_____

Six months in the future:
It is (date) _____, and I am (describe the snapshot)

_____

_____

_____

Three months in the future:
It is (date) _____, and I am (describe the snapshot)

_____

_____

_____

Step 3: Setting Your Goals

When developing your goals, make sure they meet all the criteria of the SMART method of goal setting.

Write your goals for the coming week here. These are the action items that will move you forward toward your first three-month milestone:

Goal #1:
Date to be achieved:

Goal #2:
Date to be achieved:

Goal #3:
Date to be achieved:

Goal #4:
Date to be achieved:

Goal #5:
Date to be achieved:

Be sure to create a list of goals for each week as you move toward your milestones and, ultimately, your vision. Perhaps sit down every Sunday night to review them for the upcoming week. Keep assessing them against your milestones and determine if you are on the right track. Also be sure to calendar these milestones for appropriate assessments.

In order to keep moving forward, here's what you commit to do in the next 1 to 3 months:

This is what you commit to doing in the next 3 to 6 months:

These are the steps you commit to taking in the next 6 to 12 months:

THE PURITY OF TANNA

The crimson red glow of Mount Yasur's boiling volcanic cauldron greeted us from 20 miles away as we approached the island of Tanna at night last week. Tanna is in the south islands of Vanuatu, a perplexing group of 86 islands in the South Pacific, and while it preceded our visit to Port Vila, as well as this passage from which I write, it continues to hold a tremendous impression on me.

We were there less than 24 hours, yet I can't stop thinking about its way of life. We came ashore at daybreak at Port Resolution, where Captain James Cook landed hundreds of years ago, and while the people are now dressed in modern clothing (as dirty, worn, and holey as they are), I'm not sure much else has changed since his visit. The ni-Vans, as they are called, are a deeply superstitious people, who, though having adopted Christianity, still incorporate much of the mysticism into their beliefs. And who wouldn't, given the grumbling, angry mountain so close by. But more on Mount Yasur in a bit.

We were greeted by Simon, who spoke little English and was slightly slow. Any "stranger" who enters a village in Vanuatu is escorted, due to the prevalence of "kastom" and "tabu" to ensure we walk the straight and narrow.

We were looking for Stanley, who was to be our guide to the volcano, and Simon took us to him in the village, a short walk away and past the local school, bubbling with the yells and laughter of all playgrounds worldwide. The village itself is not much different than it's been for years. Houses on stilts are still made of the forest out of wood and leaves—one room with woven leaf mats for beds. Stanley showed us how the roofs are made to ensure no water leakage, but need to be replaced every couple of years. The little groups of huts are divided into family branches, and each couple of houses share a cooking hut, with fires going and food cooking almost all the time. The younger children are running freely, ridiculously dirty, some without any pants on, playing with each other mindlessly, or hacking away with a machete at a piece of wood (!). They toss around a home-made ball made of leaves and wrapped in spider webs. As we watch, Stanley's wife quietly places three papayas into my bag and hands me a bunch of green bananas. She then brings over an impressive woven dried-leaf shoulder bag, which she holds out to me without looking me in the eye, and then quickly disappears.

Further down into the village, another clan of about a dozen men, women, and teenage boys are sitting in the midst of its group of huts on woven mats, wrapping their latest catch of fish in some sort of green leaves, and tying the leaves around with strands of dried leaves of a different kind. One of the women explains in French that they will steam the fish. Water is taken from a central spigot. And then she places five ears of corn into my bag. The corn, she explains, is thrown into the ground in special pits and left to ferment for three months. We boiled ours later that day.

The pig pen is the pride of the village. After all, pigs here stand a rung above the women as they are the only way for villagers to climb in rank. A pig kill and feast hosted by the owner is a sign of wealth and power and feeds the villagers for days. The most coveted are the males who grow tusks that circle around and painfully re-enter their jaw bones. We saw one on its way.

Later that day, we were taken to the volcano, a bumpy forty-minute four-wheel drive away, along pot-holed rutted-out paths, often along dried lava flows that naturally created the way. We arrived at the parking lot, a colorless grey, rocky expanse that seemed to go on for miles. We could have been on the moon. The climb to the crater's rim took less than 15 minutes straight up, and as we got there, the roar of the mountain made me jump. "Angry" was all I could think of. And without delay, the fireworks display began. High into the air, red hot lava spewed up, up, and up, lighting the area as if it were daylight, and then subsided again until the next rupture. All from about 300 feet away. Apparently, this is the closest one can get to the inside of a volcano anywhere in the world. And it was quite impressive.

Stanley explains that the people in Tanna believe that Mount Yasur is their creation god, and after the people prayed to him for a way to cook, he created the fire of the mountain. The people also use the boiling water that bubbles up through vents closer to the village for steaming their food, including those fresh fish that we saw being prepared. The mountain has not fully erupted in several hundred years, but has killed people who ventured too close as recently as last year. Stanley proudly explains that the people figured out the volcano's active phases far before the official government monitoring stations.

Vanuatu became a state only in 1980 (previously it was known as New Hebrides), after a mild tug-of-war between its French and British settlers. Interestingly, it was never actually colonized. The indigenous people make up over a hundred different unrelated clans, and the fact that over one hundred different local languages (not dialects) are still spoken today continues as proof. At one time, both French and British legal systems existed unofficially side-by-side (yes, people drove on both sides of the road, depending on where you came from). Still today there are remnants of this in school systems—one French and one English. The one uniting language became Bislama, a form of pigeon English...

What struck me most was the purity with which these people live. They grow whatever they need. There are no stores. There is no need for money until the school fees come due every three months, at which time the clan harvests whatever they can to sell in the big city. They all work together and share any extras with others, or it will spoil. They help each other repair roofs, wrap fish, care for children, and weave a mat. Time seems to stand still in its utmost purity.

-Barb, en route Vanuatu to Chesterfield Reef, New Caledonia
18 degrees 26.409 minutes South
164 degrees 05.324 minutes East

LESSON 5:

The Art of the Sailor:
Set Yourself Up for a Successful Crossing

The art of the sailor is to leave nothing to chance.

-Annie Van De Wiele (1922-2009)
Belgian circumnavigator

Lesson 1 has addressed the need to allow yourself to dream without censorship, even if it sounds or feels unrealistic. It taught that you must get started toward your dreams and that constant forward movement will get you there. But once you have identified your dream and you've made the commitment to live it, that's the time to come back down to earth and start your plan. That's where reality comes in.

We've learned about why we don't go after what we really want, and how to get past our pirates from Lessons 2 through 4. Notwithstanding these strategies for slaying your pirates, we also know that we don't live in a vacuum. We cannot just snap our fingers and have everything work out. It takes far more than this to achieve our dreams.

That's where Lesson 5 comes in: It teaches that it takes hard work and perseverance to keep the momentum going.

What do I need to do to set myself up for a successful leap?

Through my sailing adventures, I have identified the six steps for creating the structure that is necessary to help you take the leap toward making your dreams a reality. By taking these six steps, you will ensure that even as you navigate your pirates, you will keep pushing forward to get what you really want:

1. Put it out to the universe
2. Create a supportive crew
3. Identify your gaps
4. Create accountability
5. Create a plan and set deadlines
6. Get in touch with what has been stopping you

Sunday,
March 27,
2011

LET THE PROVISIONING BEGIN

Provisioning is the term we cruisers use when we are outfitting our boat with food. Why we don't call it grocery shopping is a mystery to me, but then so is the language sailors use for calling otherwise simple things by ridiculous names (e.g., a bathroom is a head, a bed is a berth, a kitchen is a galley, and the list goes on).

Where does one begin provisioning for a long passage? The task seemed even more overwhelming than when we left San Diego for Mexico in October of 2009. Our next *voyage will be at least three weeks long, but we need to provision for an even longer period of time since food availability is minimal in most places, and when it is available, it is pricey. My friend who is currently cruising in Australia just emailed me that a dozen eggs in the South Pacific will set us back about $6. She also blogged about spending $12 on a melon, because her crew hadn't seen fresh produce for a while.*

Back to where one starts. Several blogs and the Pacific Puddle Jumpers' website offer spreadsheets, as do several of my cruising reference books. I opted for recreating the wheel, so to speak. Well, not quite. When we came down to Mexico in October of 2009, I had created a list of things we ate for breakfast, lunch, and dinner, and shopped based on this list. The list has now become my reference sheet for provisioning. By the way, you will cook and eat on board the same way you have always cooked and eaten. Just because you've moved onto a boat, that won't change. As in, don't start buying dried beans to cook in your pressure cooker if you've never eaten dried beans before, and better yet, rarely, if ever, use your pressure cooker. Although I'd recommend you start before you move aboard, as it is so much easier on your pocket book.

Okay, again, back to where one starts. I began my provisioning this time by taking an inventory of everything I had on the boat in the way of food, cleaning and washing supplies, medicines, and toiletries. Talk about a tedious job. I was feeling depressed as Michael was crossing things off his list left and right, while I was still drowning in the hulls below the floor boards with my inventory sheet day after day. Alas, it did get completed.

From the work-of-art known as my Inventory List, for items we use often, I made an estimate of how often we eat it. For example, I make 3 cups of long grain brown rice at least once per week. Multiply this by 26 weeks and we need a lot of rice. This gets tricky, since long grain rice is hard to come by in some places in Mexico, but it is doable. For other items, I have just been winging it. Like for soy sauce, or BBQ sauce, or for so many other items. Do I get one extra bottle, or stick with what we have?

This gets even trickier since we want to be left with almost nothing by the time we make landfall in Australia in 6 to 7 months. The reason for this is that the quarantine rules are very stringent: The authorities will search your boat and take away things like fresh meat, vegetables, and dairy, but more important, any dried beans, rice and grains, plant sources, and even canned meats like tuna. Then, hopefully, a few weeks after making landfall in Australia, anything that's left must be made "gone" if we are successful in selling our dear boat there. Yet provisioning is not an exact science. And there's that psychological aspect that you MUST have enough food or YOU'LL STARVE. It has one wonder what people living on these islands eat, no?

Okay, so back to getting the provisioning started. This inventory exercise took me a full week to complete. I now have a 17 page document that lists every item on my boat, including the quantities, and where they are stored. A little overboard, perhaps, but it's done, and I'm loving the accomplishment, not to mention the system and how it works.

-Barb at Marina Riviera Nayarit, La Cruz de Huanacaxtle, Nayarit, Mexico

1. Put It Out to the Universe.

When I finally decided to share my experiences in the form of a book, my writing coach challenged me to write on my Facebook page: "I'm writing a book! What do you think about my title?" It literally took my breath away. I nearly passed out. I had now vested my Facebook friends in my process. I became accountable to them. It was no longer just me, but it became about them, as well. They know. And I don't want to disappoint. There's no better way to seal your commitment than putting your integrity at stake.

Putting out to the universe that you have made that "Whatever It Takes" decision to make a change toward following your dream will undoubtedly take your breath away.

Once you've announced it to the universe that you are on a certain path, you start noticing things you need to notice to help you on your way. There's nothing metaphysical about "sending out the vibe"— but rather now you've turned your attention and focus to what you are wanting, and that's why the doors start opening. The doors were there all along, but you just never noticed them before.

When we announced that we were going to go cruising, even though we had never owned a boat or even been on an overnight passage, we learned that there is an entire sub-culture of families who do this ... every year. There are people who are out there now who are continuing to do it. There was a wealth of information on how to get started: What boat to buy, what resources are available for home schooling, how to provision a boat, and absolutely every detail in between. This information was out there, but I never paid attention to it before.

People and resources will start falling into your lap, but not only because you are now more focused. People love being around others who are passionate about *something*. Everyone admires passion. If you go out there and share your passion, others will want to help you simply because you are passionate. We want people to achieve their goals. It simply makes the world a better place. And that makes you someone who will contribute to making the world a better place by going after your passions.

You are not the only one who is passionate about a particular topic or dream, either. By reaching out to others and revealing your passion, you will find others who share your passion. These people can collaborate, or be resources to you, and can help you on your way. They can only contribute to you living that passion, however, if they know what you are passionate about.

The exercises at the end of this chapter will help you think about how you will put it out to the universe that you are going after your dreams.

2. Create a Supportive Crew.

According to my research on what contributes to successful change, by far the most reported factor was having a supportive environment. If you want to go after something compelling and your pirates show up (and they will), you must have a good crew standing behind you and cheering you on.

To begin, become aware of who is currently part of your crew, or your circle of support. Those who are passionate about something, even something that is different than your passion, and those who are committed to reaching a goal, any goal, are good candidates for your crew. These are people who aren't afraid to dream or to work toward achieving a goal. They get what's at stake for you.

Your crew must also consist of those who are excited for you. They are your fan club, and while they may question what you are doing, they will support you, no matter what. Why is this important? Because they do not hear your pirates. They only see your greatness. They will encourage you, because they actually get how great you are.

In my small group workshops that focus on getting past those pirates, the participants spend a significant amount of time introducing themselves and saying a bit about their past life, who they are, and why they've come, or what "leap" they are wanting to make. For example, one introduction sounded like this: "Well, I was a teacher, and I didn't love, it so I became a massage therapist, and I really loved it, but then I moved abroad and stopped working, learned a second language, and now I'm back. I just don't know what my next step is." Her pirates are telling her, "You're such a flake—you can't settle down to do just one thing. Who's going to take you seriously or think you're smart or capable, given all that you've been through?"

The most interesting phenomenon occurs. Everyone else in the room sees what she's accomplished: She's managed to change gears, she's followed her dreams at least once, she's so smart to have learned another language, and so on. In fact, their own pirates are saying, "Wow. I'm not resilient enough to move abroad. I'm not smart enough to learn another language. I'm not brave enough to follow my dreams."

Someone else explains her own background: "I started out with an MBA and working in corporate finance, I got burnt out, I took some bookkeeping and accounting jobs that I hated, while I also stayed home to look after my kids, and now I'm wanting the confidence to do something more meaningful." Her pirates are telling her, "You can't cut it in the corporate world. You are a failure. You don't deserve to have a prestigious job that you love. You are not smart enough." In the meantime, everyone else hears how capable she is and recognizes her intelligence, tenacity, and ability, and they agree that she could do anything she sets her heart and mind on.

We see the strengths in others without hearing what their pirates are saying. It is essential to align yourself with people who really build you up and make you feel good about yourself, and not those who shoot you down. Surround yourself with yaysayers and not naysayers. Your crew should not be a bunch of people insisting, "You're never going to get there! You can't do this! Your dream is unrealistic!" You need to surround yourself with people who either say, "Yes, you can do it," or "I don't know *how* you're going to do it, but I trust you *will* do it."

When we started the process of looking for a boat, we contemplated the options of renting versus owning. I figured there were other people like us who didn't want to own a boat but wanted to go cruising for a period, without paying exorbitant charter rates. I wondered why I couldn't easily find boat owners who were renting out their sailboats, like homeowners rent out their vacation homes. I figured there had to be a lot of people out there trying to unload assets and settling for rental income to cover their expenses in the meantime. Perhaps there were people who were taking a break from cruising for a year. So I went online to sailing discussions and asked questions. I added that we wanted to leave in three months, would be willing to commit to renting for one year, and were open to a monohull or a catamaran. In addition, we would be willing to start on the Pacific, the Atlantic, or the Caribbean.

While there were a couple of respectful responses, the majority were rude, arrogant, and mean-spirited.

"If you are asking the question to rent out someone else's boat for a year, then I know that you're not someone I'd trust with my boat."

"I'd sooner rent out my child to you than my boat."

"Seriously, if you are asking the questions, then you know NOTHING about cruising."

"You have no clue what you are doing. You can't even make up your mind as to whether you want a monohull or a catamaran. You don't even know your cruising ground. Seriously??!"

"There's no way you'll ever start cruising in three months. Best of luck on ever getting out there."

"Come back to this list when you've done your homework."

Ultimately, we did make contact with a couple who was willing to rent out their catamaran on the Atlantic for a year while they were taking a break from cruising. We went down the path of negotiating an agreement, but realized the boat was not suitable for us. However, the point is that had we listened to the naysayers, and not sought out people who were supporting us in our dream, I wouldn't be writing this book about our adventures living on a sailboat and cruising for two-and-a-half years. And by the way, we did set out after only three months of preparation.

As an aside, if you feel excited for us that we beat the odds and the naysayers, it's a good example of what happens when you put it out to the universe and people start rooting for you.

Sunday, October 17, 2010

TOGETHERNESS (excerpts)

I must say that this has been a great time in my marriage. Who knew it would bring us so close? It certainly could have gone either way, and on many boats, it's gone south ... But for Michael and me, we've really gotten into a good groove. We work well together, and our labor divisions could not be more complementary (albeit along very traditional lines; cruisers call this the Pink and Blue jobs). We are really like a well-oiled machine when it comes to the workings of the boat and day-to-day life. We've also learned to handle each other very well when one of us is having an off day.

Like the time when we arrived in Mazatlan after being at different anchorages for about three weeks without any time alone (that's when we tend to fight the most—when we haven't spent time alone together). I had taken too much time getting ready to go out for our date night, and then got on the computer to send "one last email." Michael was furious. I still convinced him to come out with me as I also really needed to get off the boat. We went into town and had dinner outside in the town square with music playing and crowds of people. Michael sat and did not say a word the entire time, but at this point, I know he still just wanted company, and I was happy to oblige and be there for him. I was over the fight already—I get over things faster than he does. By the end of the meal, I went to the bathroom, and there I was confronted by a woman who asked me, "Are you two married?" I was startled by the question, posed completely out of the blue by a complete stranger. I responded that we were, but inquired why she had asked. She said that she and her friends watched us all night, observed that we hadn't spoken a word to each other all night and thought, "It's time for you to move on!" I had to laugh. I started blubbering amidst laughter that we live on a boat, we hadn't been alone in weeks, he's not usually like that, he's so much fun, we are very in love, blah, blah, blah. It all sounded so excuse-like, even though it was true. It turns out that this woman was the Canadian Consul General for the State of Sinaloa. And she wasn't impressed.

Interestingly, within the span of only a couple of days, both my kids asked me what makes a good marriage. I *think that, among other things, one of the most important is an admiration for the other person—for the things they do and who they are. I continue to be surprised by Michael's skill and ability in sailing this boat and keeping it in good shape. I have learned to admire and indeed enjoy his humor more than ever. He's been amazing with the kids, being a kid himself! And he's been so accommodating of my needs. I can keep going ... Bottom line, after the novelty of falling in love wears off, it's the admiration and respect you have for the other person that will keep that spark alive. For me, at least.*

-Barbara
Signing off from Isla Espiritu Santo on Playa Bonanza, Sea of Cortez, Mexico

___

We are social beings, whether we're introverted or extroverted. By nature, we need acknowledgement and championing, especially from the people around us and the people that we care about. Your crew is meant to be *your* people, *your* tribe, *your* soul-feeders. These people will keep your confidence up and help you maintain positive thinking along your route.

At the end of this chapter, you will find an exercise to assist you in putting together a list of your crew, people you will be able to count on for support as you move forward.

3. **Identify Your Gaps.**

Very few people successfully make their journey toward their dreams on their own. Almost anything we achieve is not just the result of our own hard work, but also is achieved with help and encouragement from others. Although it's not impossible to reach our goals without this help and encouragement, it will be much harder to do. Doing the things that need to get done but that are not our strengths can deplete us or become extremely time-consuming. It is, therefore, important to be able to identify your needs—where are you lacking in ability, in resources, in knowledge, and so on.

Bill Gates does not run Microsoft on his own. He has his vision, but cannot bring it to reality by taking on every role. He knows where he needs to hire out.

When I was in the middle of making a frozen lemon meringue cake and needed a way to scorch the topping because I didn't have a broiler to my oven, I got on the VHF radio in our anchorage and put out a call for anyone who may have a blow torch. Surprisingly, someone did.

This is not the same as when your pirates show up to say you don't know how to do something. Identifying the gaps in what you need to accomplish your goal is simply a logistical issue. Filling that gap with the help of another will strengthen your journey toward getting what you want.

In other words, if you don't know how to adjust your sail, you need to have people who can either teach you or who can do it for you.

Sunday,
October 17,
20110

TOGETHERNESS (excerpts)

If there is one word I could use to describe our relationships aboard Whatcha Gonna Do this past year, it would be "togetherness." There is no doubt that it takes a certain kind to be able to endure so much togetherness living in small quarters with little escape 24 hours a day, 7 days a week. I would not have said I was that type, but I seemed to overlook this factor when we decided to do this trip. I was awed by the opportunity to do something different, exciting, adventurous, and fun. I knew it would be a lot of work, and I had my reservations about homeschooling the kids when I felt challenged simply helping them with homework. Perhaps these side-tracked me from the fact that I have always needed my personal space and independence. I love my "Me Time."

Besides, when I'm at home and I have my "ugly" moments, I can go off and be by myself. No one has to see it. Not so when you are together ALL THE TIME. At those times of ugliness, I can't stand myself, so I can't imagine how the others feel about me. And at times like that, I just need my space. My sweet kids take it as a time to want to comfort me (Michael knows better by now), and I have to tell them that for the moment, I just want to be by myself, assuring them that I'll be alright.

In this small space, where does one go? To the bow of the boat, to my room with the fans blowing, to shore for a walk if it's not too hot, for a swim, for a kayak. One needs to get creative.

In the book by Janna Cawrse Esarey, "The Motion of the Ocean," the author states that it's not so much the togetherness, but rather the lack of "otherness." Your crewmates have to be everything to you. Which is pretty impossible. I don't think any one person can be everything to you. In fact, I think that's unhealthy. So it gets a bit tricky when we are somewhere or en route somewhere alone. What you must know, however, is that we are rarely alone. There is one wonderful cruising community out there. We have made some good friends along the way, so we have found alternative venues for "sharing" (aka complaining) when the need arises. The things we (read: women) complain about are understood by every other cruiser (female) out there, regardless of age, background, education, or culture. The men, on the other hand, only need to discuss alternators, converters, sail drives, pumps and the like, and they'll be fine. That and a partner to come home to, and voila: Needs met.

...

Then there are the kids ... I am not sure how other families do it when they have young kids. At least we all get breaks from each other. And it's far from being bad. Indeed, it's been mostly great. We have bonded as a family unit. We have many game nights and organized family outings, like snorkeling or hiking. We slept on the trampoline together on the hot summer nights. Finally, a bed big enough for all of us! And then there are the moments, so many I can't count, of great times that just happen when we are just being together. Today, we helped each other as we caught two fish at the same time – all four of us taking turns reeling them in on two rods, excited to see what we had caught. We've had great conversations about issues like the BP oil spill and the

Holocaust. The kids get to share interesting facts as they do their school work.

My relationships with each one separately have flourished. How decadent to be able to really get to know your kids – through how they learn, to how they think and what they are curious about. Of course, I love them, but with each day, as I learn more about them, and from them, I realize, "Hey, I really like them as people."

...

The issues on board a cruising boat don't seem much different on land, except that they are magnified, given the close quarters, and, of course, the lack of other distractions like work or school. Creativity in finding that otherness and/or that personal space is the key. Some days it works, and some days, not so much.

-Barbara
Signing off from Isla Espiritu Santo on Playa Bonanza, Sea of Cortez, Mexico

The end of this chapter contains an exercise to help you begin thinking about the gaps in your knowledge, ability, and/or resources. The creation of this list is a work in progress as you add your needs as you go. The list will most certainly require amendments and additions along the way. It will hopefully work for you as a catalyst for thinking differently about enlisting resources to help you get to where you want to go. And be sure to look at it as a strength when you can identify where you need help.

4. Create Accountability.

One of the best ways to keep moving forward is through accountability, which is essential to your success. When you are accountable to someone else, just like when you put it out to the world, your integrity is at stake. It ensures you have done what you said you were going to do.

There are many ways to set up an accountability plan. You can work with a life coach, who is trained to help you achieve your goals and listens for resonance as you set your milestones. A good coach will hold you accountable for what you say you're going to do, and if you don't, he or she will examine why and help you make the necessary adjustments.

Another option is to create your own formalized accountability group of like-minded people who you respect, who are positive do-ers, and who have similar goals of making a change. This group may or may not be the same as your crew, as the two serve different purposes. The members of your accountability group are people who want support to reach their own goals and who are supportive in championing you to reach your own. The group must meet regularly for the purpose of assessing goals and milestones. This group would design with each other how they want you to be in holding them accountable, and vice versa. Each member of your group will develop his or her own plan (as noted in Step 5 below). You may choose to begin with each member creating his/her own vision, setting his/her own milestones, and then setting out what steps each must take by the next meeting toward reaching each person's own goals.

Exercises are provided at the end of this chapter for developing an accountability group.

5. Create a Plan and Set Deadlines.

So many people move through life without really knowing where they're going or why they're doing what they are doing. They have no plan. That's why the starting point for any plan is made with the end in mind. You must first commit to your endpoint, or dream, even if the dream seems, well, dreamy. The key to remember is that if you don't know where you're heading, you won't know how to get there.

Once you have your destination, you can create the navigation plan. While the navigation toward your port can change depending on the weather as you move forward, you must at least begin with a course in mind.

Saturday, March 19, 2011 | **MAKING THE DECISION**

So here we are. Our cruising plans have changed several times. We started out on a one-year plan, which has extended into two, and then into a few more months beyond that. We started out planning to be in Central America in the first year and didn't make it, and then planned to make it there in the second year, and then changed our minds. We thought we'd head to the South Pacific, and then weren't sure we should do that, given that we'd need to extend another few months ... [The kids were convinced that the South Pacific is where we should be going.]...

Now Michael and I had to decide if we were ready. "Ready" is a subjective word. Our boat is undoubtedly ready. But are we? Mentally? Interestingly, I am thoroughly looking forward to the three-week passage, with nothing to do but homeschool, hang out and play games with my kids, do art projects, do yoga, read, write plenty of blogs, and sleep. In addition to being on watch 24/7 (on a schedule of course, sharing it with the rest of my crew). There's no shopping, laundry, dates, Internet, or other distractions. We'll be completely present. But once we get there??? It's a completely different type of cruising than we've been doing. Passages between the islands are usually three to seven days. Most of the anchorages are trickier due to coral heads, cones, and the like. You are clearly much more off the beaten track, and what if we need emergency help? Internet connections are spotty and scarce. Fresh produce is even scarcer in many of the destinations. And if you could get past all of the above, there are SHARKS that swim in the anchorages in the Marquesas.

On the other hand, all this is so exciting, and a once in a lifetime experience—for all of us. Other people have managed to overcome all of the above, so why can't we?

So we took a deep breath and plunged in. We've now set our schedule to depart around April 1, just so that we have a deadline. We're going to the South Pacific ... unless, of course, we decide not to between now and then ...

-Barb
La Cruz de Huanacaxtle, Nayarit, Mexico

There's a saying that goes: "A sailor's plan is written in the sand at low tide." It is important not to get so rigid, or so committed to the plan, that there is no room to make changes to it. The need may arise to make slight adjustments, or big ones. Things may happen that feel like failure, but they are only there as a knock on the hull to say, "Hey, it's time to change direction." The sure thing is that adjustments will need to be made along the way.

Nonetheless, deadlines need to be made. Without deadlines, your "to-do" list will only remain a "some-day" list.

We have addressed the concept of creating a plan and setting deadlines, together with the accompanying exercises, in Lesson 4, by creating your "to-do" list in the form of single actionable steps (your goals) that support your journey toward your dream (or your vision). It also addresses the in-between steps (your milestones) used to assess whether you are still on the right course or require a shift to realign yourself with your dream. The result is a compelling plan that will excite and inspire you.

6. Get in Touch with What Has Been Stopping You.

That's where Lessons 2 through 4 came in. Getting beyond your pirates is truly core to following your dreams.

A lot of people ask me if I were shipwrecked, and could only have one book, what would it be? I always say, "How to Build a Boat."

-Stephen Wright (1955-)
American comedian, actor, writer

EXERCISE:
Putting It Out to the Universe

I will commit to putting out to the universe what I am doing by:

- ☐ Posting on Facebook, LinkedIn, or other social media site.
- ☐ Tweeting about it.
- ☐ Talking to __ (number) people per week about it.
- ☐ Blogging about it.
- ☐ Other: _____

EXERCISE:
Creating a Supportive Crew

These are the people I can count on in my life who will support me and encourage me:

These are the people in my life who will be naysayers and deplete me:

EXERCISE:
Identifying Your Gap

These are the resources that I must acquire in order to move forward on my path:

Things I don't yet know:

Talent I must farm out:

Amount of money I may need:

Other resources I think I need:

EXERCISE:
Setting Up an Accountability Group

List the people you'd like to have in your accountability group based on the criteria noted in this chapter:

List what you will need from the group to achieve your goals (e.g., hard truth-telling or gentle reminders):

How often do you want to meet and where?

Who will run the meetings? The same person or on a rotating basis?

What is the format for these meetings? Informal, or everyone gets a certain amount of time for the group to focus on that individual?

A (MOSTLY) HAPPY
END TO 2011

It's taken me a while to start typing this blog, as I'm not really sure what to say, even after being home for nearly a week. We're trying to take re-entry slowly, keeping a pace familiar to boaters in which we don't schedule too much, we don't rush too much, and we enjoy our time together just "hanging."

The first thing that struck me was how good it is to be back. We live in perhaps one of the best places in the world. There is no doubt something special about blue skies and sunshine (even if the air feels a bit crispy) that lifts one's spirit. The scenery is spectacular. (I reached my favorite spot on my favorite hike today which showcases the mountains and the bay.) And my community here is like none other. I love my friends. Period.

Next, I am trying not to be too overwhelmed by all the activity. Sounds a bit trite to say, but there are a lot of cars on the roads. (I'm driving steadily again after 2.5 years.) I am connected to Internet and cell phones again, and people really expect that you will respond instantaneously to emails and calls. I do not have texting, and, at this point, don't anticipate getting it—that would simply send me over the top. Going from technology disconnect to being connected again is perhaps the biggest adjustment. And there is so much to buy. Shopping has a much different perspective when one lives on a small boat; there's not much room for anything more than what you really need, and that is refreshing.

As for my kids, they are forced to take re-entry slowly, since many of their friends are away this break. Danielle, although a bit nervous, is elated to be home and anticipating being with a steady flow of kids with a giddiness I haven't seen in a long time. Harrison is a bit more anxious, and I'm assuming this is because he was so young when we left that he's really not sure what to expect. They've spent hours watching TV and have even been okay going shopping for clothes (of which they had very few upon arrival).

In many ways, we are returning; in other ways, we are the new kids and things seem a bit strange.

As for Whatcha Gonna Do, our home for the last 2.5 years, I do miss her and the way she took care of us—something we tend to take for granted when we live in a house. What I do not miss is the waking in the middle of almost every night to close hatches or listen for an odd sound. And I am enjoying my showers and non-marine-type toilets. I am looking forward to some routine, especially once school starts next Tuesday, we move back into our house sometime next week, and Michael rejoins us stateside in a couple of weeks.

But I will sadly miss many friends, the lifestyle, and adventure travel we have been so fortunate to have grown so accustomed to.

Happy 2012 to all of our family and our friends, new and old. We thank you for following our adventures with us, but the next chapter is just beginning. I can't wait to see what this year brings.

-Barb
from Palo Alto, CA

CONCLUSION:
My Truth

Cruising has two pleasures. One is to go out in wider waters from a sheltered place. The other is to go into a sheltered place from wider waters.

--Howard Bloomfield
Author

We returned from our nearly two-and-a-half year sailing adventure in January of 2012. Before moving back into our house, we used the opportunity to do some painting and decorating to create a haven for ourselves, while streamlining our possessions to only those items we really felt we needed. We landscaped. We refreshed inside and out.

My children returned to school at the half-way mark following the winter break. Danielle returned to the second half of eighth grade, her first time in middle school. She went from being a girl when she left after fifth grade to looking and acting like a beautiful mature woman. She was thrilled to be with her old friends and academically finished her year with stellar grades. She entered high school that fall with a renewed appreciation for having loads of kids around and has been on the honor roll ever since.

Harrison returned to enter the second half of fifth grade. He was slightly more uncertain. It seemed that more change occurred socially among his classmates from when he left after second grade than Danielle experienced going from fifth to eighth grade. Nonetheless, after a couple of months, he was once again feeling like he belonged, and by the time he entered middle school in the fall, I realized that he was completely on track socially—he was texting his friends and telling me not to hang around. Academically, he was right where he should have been and at the head of his class in several subjects. His biggest observation about the change from cruising to life on land was that he was now spending close to seven hours a day at school and still having homework to do once he got home, versus homeschooling when we got his work done in the morning's four hours and was free to explore for the rest of the day. And he's making up for lost time on the computer, his real passion.

Clearly my fears about destroying my kids by taking them cruising were completely unfounded.

My husband, Michael, came back and hit the ground running. He did what he's always done. He networked, he worked on deals, he was busy. After a few months, he was invited to join a small financial services firm, where he continues to work doing what he loves: Deal-making. What changed in him, however, was the way in which he approaches life. He is far calmer about what the future holds and continues to have a much greater appreciation for where life takes him. Together, we have learned that anything is possible, if we allow ourselves to dream.

It took a year to sell our boat in Australia, which was one of our fears. In the end, however, it all worked out. We believe we got a fair price, and it's bittersweet that *Whatcha Gonna Do* now belongs to another cruising family.

As for me, I spent about ten months just taking it all in, trying to figure out what had changed in me. I maintained my friendships with all my good friends, even while I hadn't regularly kept in touch with many of them along the way. It's not surprising, however, that they stuck around. After all, they have been part of my own crew all along.

While I still continue to be mostly the same person, I feel much bolder and have far fewer fears. I started up my coaching practice again, serving individual clients at a crossroads, wanting to make their next steps really count. I coach with a purpose and for each client's cause. I re-initiated my Women's Career Strategy Workshops that bring real-life possibilities for women wanting to find a meaningful and sustainable career. The aliveness these women bring to the table as they begin to allow themselves to dream is perhaps one of the most fulfilling experiences I have had since I've returned to land. I have been invited to speak to groups about my parallel journeys—sailing through the Pacific, and sailing to my own success, slaying my pirates and toward my vision. I have used these stories, and especially the principles behind slaying pirates, as I coach my clients, facilitate workshop participants, and address audiences of all sizes. And I still can't believe that it's all been part of the vision I had created for myself years ago.

In the face of my pirates, we survived—physically and emotionally—and we are not destitute! We have grown through our experiences. We feel much bolder in our actions to go after what we really want. We feel accomplished and have a sense of contentment that we have never had before. We believe in the power of the dream and in going after it.

What I've also discovered is that once we have achieved our goals, it takes work to stay there and maintain the aliveness that has come as a result of our achievements. There is a famous quote that I love by British novelist Hammond Innes (1937-1998): "He who lets the sea lull him into a sense of security is in very grave danger." We cannot become complacent to being on our way. We must always be vigilant about what we want in our lives on a continuing basis. I'm certainly willing to put the work in to keep going. I've seen the benefits already.

Here's what I know to be true:

Your life is a gift. Living it as it was meant to be lived is a duty. If you are going to sail to your own success, you must choose to live as your best, fullest, highest self. That person lives inside of you; and until you live according to that self's purpose, only you will know the impact that self *could* have. You owe it not just to yourself, but to all of us, and to whatever God or other spirit that you adhere to (or not), to live according to who you were meant to be.

Only you get to choose whether you'll go after what you really want, or not. If you feel like taking a sailing adventure is too big for right now, get the idea in motion by putting it out to the world that you're dreaming of doing it, then be amazed at what you notice starts coming your way—not because of fate, but because you've now opened yourself up to noticing and to receiving.

Don't go it alone—no successful person ever has. Develop your own crew of excited supporters and motivation through accountability groups to keep you on track. Identify where you need to farm out tasks. Do things you love to do that make you feel fulfilled and, therefore, much bolder than you otherwise would feel. Take chances.

Get in touch with what's been stopping you and realize how silly most of those pirates are. Create your vision for who you want to be, and by setting your course toward that vision, you will undoubtedly get closer to living your dreams, on purpose and aligned with who you really and truly are.

And be prepared to make adjustments along the way—not because of failures, but because of the assessments you've needed to make.

Perhaps the most important step to take, however, is the first one. It's setting your course into action. It's cutting your bowlines. It's just getting a move on. Charter a boat for a weekend. Join a crew on a sailing rally. Get yourself to a foreign destination and experience it for a while. But get moving. Get started. See where it takes you.

My own real journey didn't begin with a two-and-a-half year sailing journey or even when my husband proposed the idea. It began with the thought of writing a book. My own pirates were telling me I shouldn't do it for far too many reasons to recount. Until I stopped to hear their nonsense, I was not going to sail to my own version of success. Until I created a compelling vision for myself that has me sharing the principles contained in this book with more people so they can go out and be the best that they are, I was never even going to begin the writing process. Once I did make the first step, resources and opportunities came my way. And I've been slaying pirates the entire way.

If you are indeed reading this, you'll know that my pirates were dead wrong.

The sail, the play of its pulse so like our own lives; so thin and yet so full of life, so noiseless when it labors hardest, so noisy and impatient when least effective.

-Henry David Thoreau (1817-1862)
American author, poet and philosopher

ACKNOWLEDGEMENTS

We are all inventors, each sailing out on a voyage of discovery, guided each by a private chart, of which there is no duplicate. The world is all gates, all opportunities.

-Ralph Waldo Emerson (1883-1882)
American essayist, lecturer and poet

No author does it alone. It is with deep gratitude that I thank the following for contributing to my success:

My numerous clients and workshop participants, who have taught me a thing or two about resilience, inspiration, and success;

My numerous teachers at Coaches Training Institute (www.thecoaches.com), who have helped me find my calling and have sent me off to co-actively create.

My many friends, who cheered me on from the moment I announced I would write a book and have been with me every step of the way. In particular, Beth Blecherman, Techmama (www.techmamas.com), author mama, blogger mama, inspiration mama, has taken me for reality walks and encouragement journeys.

Cindy Walsh, my project manager at Bush Street Press, who kept me on track, work-wise and sanity-wise.

Alicia Dunams, my writing coach and a luminary in the field of writing books (www.aliciadunams.com).

Madeleine Payamps, my personal coach and friend, who is brilliant beyond compare (womenintransitioncoach.com).

My mom, Freda Gottesman-Brender, a mathematician and, therefore, a woman of numbers, yet perhaps the smartest person I know on human relationships and living a life of strong moral character. You have taught me the power in laughing at myself. You have been beside me with support, compassion, love, and lots of laughter (as well as advice!) whenever and wherever I've been in my life.

My sister, Maureen Gottesman, who tirelessly acted as editor, cook, caregiver, babysitter, and cheerleader.

My sister, Deborah Gottesman, who always hears me out, believes in me, and makes me laugh like no one else.

My children, Danielle and Harrison, for putting up with days on end of writing, or trying to write, and neglecting everything else, so I could meet my deadlines, yet still came in every night to hug and kiss me goodnight. It is for you that I do what I do: my hopes and dreams for you both is that you live with purpose, passionately, with love and appreciation for your blessings, and with tremendous fulfillment.

Last, but certainly not least, to my husband, Michael, who rocks my world each and every day, who complements me beautifully and compliments me daily, who encourages me when I feel like there's no more energy left, who makes me laugh when I take myself too seriously, who believes in me sometimes more than even I believe in myself, and with whom I am deeply in love.

-Barbara Gottesman
May, 2013

I find the great thing in this world is not so much where we stand, as in what direction we are moving: To reach the port of heaven, we must sail sometimes with the wind and sometimes against it – but we must sail, and not drift, nor lie at anchor.

-Oliver Wendel Holmes (1841-1935)
U.S. Supreme Court Justice

ABOUT THE AUTHOR

Barbara Gottesman spent two-and-a-half years sailing with her husband and two children through Mexico, the South Pacific, and Australia, realizing a lifetime family travel dream. All four of them survived.

As a certified life coach serving high achievers wanting to make their next step really count, Barbara has been called the "ultimate connector," bringing together ideas, thoughts, beliefs, and feelings, to create the tools for making change. Her work has been described by her clients as "empowering" and "life changing." Her website, www.BGCoaching.com, keeps you up-to-date on what she's doing, contains links to her inspiring and informative coaching blog, and allows you to stay in touch with her via newsletter.

No stranger to making big changes, Barbara was a practicing attorney for ten years, founded a cooking school aimed at healthy eating for young families, has made international and cross-country moves, and seeks adventure travel. Surprisingly, she doesn't consider herself intrinsically adventurous.

Barbara currently lives in Menlo Park, CA, with her husband and two children. She can be reached at Barb@BGCoaching.com.